Florence Hers

There is an immense hunger for the help this book offers. In CRY PAIN, CRY HOPE we have an unparalleled guide for understanding the various dimensions of call. For a growing person, call must continue forever to be the central concern. At each evolving level of our being we are asking: "What am I going to do with my life now?" "How do I hear call?" "How do I find the vocation that is related to my deepest self, and will help that self to unfold?" Every facet of the personality is included in the answer to these questions. Thus the wide range of topics covered by the author. One of the important insights in the book is that the person who has found the work that is his or hers to do is at play in the world. Play and vocation are one.

N. Gordon Cosby, Minister
Church of the Saviour
Washington, D.C.

ELIZABETH O'CONNOR

CRY PAIN, CRY HOPE

Thresholds to Purpose

WORD BOOKS
PUBLISHER
WACO, TEXAS

A DIVISION OF
WORD, INCORPORATED

The chapter, "The Thinking Heart," was previously published and is reprinted with
permission from *Sojourners*, Box 29272, Washington, D.C. 20017. Poem on page 27
of *The Irrational Season* by Madeleine L'Engle, copyright © 1977 by Crosswicks,
Ltd., is reprinted by permission of Harper & Row, Publishers, Inc. "The Poor
House" is reprinted with permission of Macmillan Publishing Company from *Collected Poems* by Sara Teasdale, copyright © 1915 by Macmillan Publishing Company,
renewed 1943 by Mamie T. Wheless. Lines from "Mass for the Day of St. Thomas
Didymus," from *Candle in Babylon* by Denise Levertov, copyright © 1982 by Denise
Levertov, and lines from *The Poet in the World* by Denise Levertov, copyright © 1973
by Denise Levertov Goodman, are reprinted by permission of New Directions Publishing Corporation.

Unless otherwise indicated, Scripture quotations are from the *Jerusalem Bible*, copyright © 1966 by Darton, Longman & Todd, Ltd. and Doubleday and Company, Inc.
Used by permission of the publisher.

Additional Scripture quotations are from the following sources: The *New English
Bible* (NEB), © The Delegates of The Oxford University Press and the Syndics of The
Cambridge University Press, 1961, 1970. Reprinted by permission. The *Revised
dard Version of the Bible* (RSV), copyrighted 1946, 1952, © 1971, 1973 by the Division
of Christian Education of the National Council of the Churches of Christ in the
U.S.A., and used by permission.

Library of Congress Cataloging-in-Publication Data:

O'Connor, Elizabeth.
    Cry pain, cry hope.

    1. Christian life—1960–   . I. Title.
BV4501.2.O316 1987   248.4   87-10416
ISBN 0-8499-0618-0

7898 BKC 987654321

Printed in the United States of America

For Kathleen, my sister of
noble and gentle heart

I wish to develop my reflections further,
they fill me as full as the moon at the full.
Ecclesiasticus 39:12

Contents

Acknowledgments

At the completion of every book I find myself in the debt of love, a fact that makes me grateful to the Apostle Paul for his injunction "Avoid getting into debt, except the debt of mutual love" (Rom. 13:8). This Scripture comforts my heart when I think of what I owe to Dorothy Devers who has edited so many of my books. Dorothy is the author of a small volume entitled *Faithful Friendship*. She knows whereof she speaks for she is herself a faithful friend whose help and caring my writings always need.

To Maryle Ashley, Sunny and Bill Branner, who considered this manuscript in its typed form and encouraged me to publish it, I am also in debt. Among my other creditors are Mary Anders, who tracked down books for me, and Larry Gingrich, who helped with the typing. All writers should have the kind of support these friends gave.

Love is due as well to my church community for the setting in which to write and, more importantly, for not reproaching me for the times when I am not as present to them as I might be.

In addition, there are those mentioned by name in this book. In varied ways our paths intersected and I am in the debt of each one of them. Among these certainly should be included Nikolai Berdyaev, Simone Weil, Dietrich Bonhoeffer, Etty Hillesum, and Joseph Campbell whose influence can be noted in these pages and whose writings continue to expand my knowledge and vision of the world.

Finally, I am in the debt of the folk at Word Books who have believed in me over the years and been willing to take the risks of love.

Preface

The selections in this book were written over a five-year period. The underlying theme is vocation, or "call," as we refer to it in my community of The Church of The Saviour, Washington, D.C. Whenever this subject surfaced in me I found myself deserting my jottings in a journal to develop the theme more fully. What I had intended as an entry in a journal would become an essay. I considered organizing this loose collection of seemingly random prose into a less personal and more orderly book on the subject of "call." In the end I decided against this, although the book is more uneven in design and pace than it otherwise would have been. The writings, as they now appear, enable the reader to see how I worked with the matter of call even when I was unaware of it. I must admit that Gordon Cosby, Minister of the Church of the Saviour and my friend and mentor in such matters, encouraged me to let the pieces stand as they were written. While he agreed that something is gained in the more conceptual and abstract statement, something is lost when we do not tell each other the story of how it was for us, and with us, when we took seriously the truths about which we preach and write.

The journey from the head to the heart, as we all know, is the longest distance we will ever cover. As we make that journey individually and corporately it often seems disjointed, not thematic. In looking back we discover that the unifying theme is call. When I wrote about the old woman on Columbia Road I did not know that she had anything to do with Sarah's Circle, the vision I would describe much later and which would enlist me fully in its service. Similarly, when writing about money I did not know how much our fearful hold on money, possessions, and comforts keeps us from responding to call. Only in rereading these writings did I learn that day by day and month by month we are given the inner and outer experiences that contain God's address to us.

Every single one of us has a "good work" to do in life. This good work not only accomplishes something needed in the world, but completes something in us. When it is finished a new work emerges that will help us to make green a desert place, as well as to scale another mountain in ourselves. The work we do in the world, when it is true vocation, always corresponds in some mysterious way to the work that goes on within us. It is a "green work" and a "greening work," to use the insightful words of Hildegard of Bingen. Matthew Fox, who has given us wonderful new books on her writings and paintings, states that Hildegard refers to God's greening power as wetness. We are all to stay "wet and moist, like God." The opposite is too terrible—to become "shrivelled and wilted."[1]

With each new stage of life a new work emerges in us. In all likelihood it was there from the beginning, waiting to be claimed, waiting for the development of our personalities and of our gifts. We are probably intended to embark upon a new work, or a new dimension of an old work, every seven years. This suggests the Jubilee cycle which incorporated the understanding that the seventh year, like the seventh day, marked the completion of a work, and that even the spent land would need a period of rest before being able to yield new fruits. Vocation is always deeply related to those changes that take place in us on our journey toward the freedom to be our true selves, God's word and work in the universe.

The transition stage—the time between works—is often signaled by growing feelings of discontent. The work we have been doing ceases to absorb us in the same way. Finally it seems impossible to endure until the weekend, or vacation, or retirement. The period is one of anxiety, sometimes experienced as boredom. One reaches toward the new without knowing what the new is. The transition stage is a difficult period because the old has lost its meaning, the new has not yet loomed into sight, and one has serious doubts that it will come at all. These thoughts cause varying degrees of unrest and, in the extreme, despair. There is nothing to do but wait, and waiting is something few of us do well. We find ourselves, as it were, in exile. Only when looking back do we see that the pain was part of the design, seeking to pull us into the new. Pain kept us open in our waiting—asking, listening, looking, willing to make that journey into self—a journey few of us undertake with any seriousness until compelled by our suffering.

When I began to record the thoughts in this book I did not realize I was in a transition stage, so lost was I in the outer scene. I thought I was keeping a journal to record the creativity that was bursting out all around me. All of it was happening because people were taking seriously the matter of their individual calls and the corporate call of the community. I wanted to share the week-by-week experience of living in the midst of new adventures unfolding in order to witness to creativity— the call that transcends all the individual expressions of call. With my sister Hildegard, I yearned for the whole world to know that God had "exalted humankind with the vocation of creation."[2] To my surprise, however, I found I was writing of other concerns. I was also feeling like an outsider. When you are surrounded by people hearing call and responding to call, being in a transition stage is especially lonely. "If I let go of what I have and what I know, will there be a place for me?" is the fearful question hovering over every new stage of the journey. And how does one speak to confident and "busy ones" of such matters without feeling odd or inferior?

Call has many facets because the whole of life coheres around it. If we are to make ultimate sense of our lives, all the disparate elements in us have to be integrated around call. The whole life of Jesus revolved around call, as did the life of Moses before him. The theme was in their lives as it is in the life of each of us. We have to deal with it or we become narrow and restrictive, the inevitable price of turning one's back on call—

an option that is always present. My hope is that this book will invite the reader to work more consciously with call in his or her own life, and that the different selections will suggest ways of hearing and responding to call.

When we honor call in our lives, we honor it in the lives of others and of our institutions, for institutions—like people—journey by stages. They, too, must die to the old in order to be born to the new. The failure of an institution to follow its commitment to creativity causes it to wither and die—to become full of dead men's bones. A structure intended for the healing of the common life changes into a vehicle of oppression. Perhaps, when vocation becomes a more conscious consideration in our individual lives, it will become a more conscious consideration in our corporate life as the people of God called to freedom and creativity.

1

On Writing

A book stirs in me, but enormous resistances in myself must be overcome, if ever I am to give it form. I wonder whether that is not always the creator's experience before a new work. Certainly the resistances within me have grown greater with each new book. Partly I am undone by what I feel to be the expectations of others. I think that, if I set aside a portion of my day for writing, at the end of that day some evidence of my industry will be demanded of me. This attitude became clear when friends, asking me to spend a week with them in New Hampshire, said for enticement, "You can use your mornings to write." Immediately came the picture of their waiting outside my door each afternoon to see the typed pages. Hemmed in by that image I knew that I would be too anxious to produce anything, and that the week would go by with nothing "to show" for my solitary labor.

It is as though I am slave labor—back in Egypt building tombs. Conditions in my slave camp, however, seem worse because I do not know that I can produce the work that my camp overseers demand. Interrupting that thought to check the Scriptures, I discovered that the Hebrews in Egypt were in the same predicament, not knowing whether they could meet the demand made of them.

The overseers and foremen went out and said to the people, "Pharaoh's orders are that no more straw is to be supplied. Go and get it for yourselves wherever you can find it; but there will be no reduction in your daily task." So the people scattered all over Egypt to gather stubble for straw, while the overseers kept urging them on, bidding them complete, day after day, the same quantity as when straw was supplied (Exod. 5:10–14, NEB).

How oppressive that situation was, and to think that I make for myself that kind of intolerable atmosphere, and perceive my friends and community as overseers and foremen! I am trying to gather my projections back into myself and find the inner Pharaohs that drive me in such unrelenting ways.

In stark contrast to my own is a story that Peter Stitt tells about Flaubert:

Some friends came by his house on Friday to ask if he would join them on a weekend picnic. He said no, he was much too busy. They looked at his manuscript, made some small talk, and went on their way. On Sunday night they came back to say what a wonderful time they had had. They also asked Flaubert how his work had gone. He said that he had made enormous progress. So they looked at the manuscript again, and noticed that he was at exactly the same point as on Friday—in the middle of a sentence interrupted by a comma. They chided him for making no progress at all. He replied that they didn't understand—that he had, on Saturday changed the comma to a semicolon, and on Sunday changed it back to a comma; thus he had made wonderful progress.[3]

Long time for brooding marks a life free of Pharaoh's rule.

2

I Am Who I Am

Scripture comes alive for me these days. I am rereading the Book of Exodus and making all kinds of fresh discoveries. Justice, truth, freedom—these are the great words of this book. I see myself as both the oppressed and the oppressor. I am afraid of freedom, afraid of the risks—of losing the people I depend on, of losing the community I love, the attention I think I need, the approval I cannot live without. Ambiguous in my feelings—unwilling to pretend, but fearful of honesty. Wanting to conform to whatever is the current definition of servanthood, virtue, Christian, and at the same time wanting to find my own definitions, to set myself free.

The only way to understand Exodus is to make real those events in one's own life—to take the risks of freedom.

What are those risks?

For me they are all summed up in rejection—that most painful of all feelings. If I openly follow my path I have friends who will learn that their hearts are not in communion with mine. We all seek out the company of those who think the way we think and perceive the world the way we perceive it. It is when we find an at-oneness with each other that we feel at home, accepted, companioned. I am afraid of seeing what others do not see, or hearing what they do not hear. I want to be in step with the people I care about, to laugh with them, celebrate with them, and agree with them. In all the world I want least to be a prophet. Perhaps this is the way it is with everyone, and may be the reason we have so few prophets. Yet it is a vocation that is dangerous to refuse because it means that we will either conform to others or insist that they conform to us—the oppressed or the oppressor. To be truly human includes a willingness to say one's own word and to allow others to say their own word.

No wonder God instructed Moses to tell the people, "I Am has sent me to you" (Exod. 3:14). Who but the God of the liberation movement would have given such a message to the people in bondage, "I Am who I Am" (Exod. 3:14) or "I will be who I will be." These are the words that address my own temptation to slavery. These are the words that support my day-to-day struggle to be who I am.

3

Moses—Paradigm for Vocation

All over the world suffering people are holding in their hands the Book of Exodus, and finding hope as they struggle for freedom against the backdrop of its pages. This is the book I see most often mentioned when reading about the Basic Ecclesial Communities of the poor that have sprung up throughout Brazil and most of the continent of South America. The Exodus story that looms so large in the history of American blacks, and finds its way into the Gospel music of the South, is now giving inspiration and spirit to the small churches born of the poor in Central America.

Pondering the pages of Exodus is a way of understanding Christian vocation, and a way of drawing close to Jesus Christ. I like to think that all through his life Jesus held this book in his hands and let its words sink into his being, his imagination captured then, as mine is now, by the gigantic figure of Moses that dominates its pages. We find the name of Moses in the mouth of Jesus and, in all, appearing thirty-seven times in the Gospels and forty-seven more in the other New Testament books. In Revelation are these words:

They all had harps from God, and they were singing the hymn of Moses, the servant of God, and of the Lamb (Rev. 15:3).

We can be confident that Jesus sat with his family at the Passover table and asked in his turn the question that every elder son asks the father on that night, "What does this mean?" and that Joseph gave the wondrous answer Moses instructed him to give, "By sheer power Yahweh brought us out of Egypt, out of the house of slavery" (Exod. 13:14).

The story of Moses, as we all know, begins in the land of Egypt. In the unfolding of that story one glimpses how the individual events in the life of Moses intersected with the events of world history and prepared his heart to hear God's call upon his life. In all likelihood Moses' ancestors were a nomadic people who had to keep on the move in order to find food. Finally famine drove them into the Fertile Crescent land of the pharaohs where they were allowed to settle. In time their number grew; they prospered and gained power, making them a threat to those who were worrying about economics, their own future, and foreigners taking over. A climate of hospitality changed to one of greed and fear.

The Hebrews were enslaved and put to work building the cities of the empire. This might have eased Pharaoh's heart had not the Jews, like all oppressed people, had more and more babies. One would think they would have known better, but it always seems that the harder life becomes for poor and stricken people, the more babies they have. Pharaoh, feeling even more insecure, made their working conditions harsher. He flogged them, accused them of being lazy, and made them work longer hours. This story is not unlike accounts from the cotton fields of the South and the garment factories of the North, and the stories we read each week about the poor of the world.

A recent news item reports that a half million migrant U. S. farm workers have lost a thirteen-year fight to compel growers to provide work-site toilet and wash facilities. Although poor sanitation and related diseases are second only to poverty in the list of miseries that afflict the farm workers, no one with the power to effect change has listened with the ears of the heart as an oppressed people have tried to put their mute sufferings into words.

In Pharaoh's Egypt the abusive language and cruel treatment of the Israelites had its effect—self-scorn, inertia, and despondency. People who work hard and are denied the critical minimum of food and housing, told often enough that they are lazy and will amount to nothing, come to believe it. That is the decisive outcome of oppression. People living in dehumanizing conditions become, to our surprise, less than human. The crowded prisons and constant allocations for larger, better jails reflect the trouble we are in as a society. The methods used to deal with those who have been brutalized, and have themselves become brutal, are to tighten the control and increase the punishment, further confirming their self-hatred and dependency.

The oppressive working conditions that existed in Pharaoh's Egypt prevail in every part of the world today. All over this globe men and women are at hard labor the whole day long for wages that barely allow them to survive. As for the jobless, we have so often heard the statistics that we no longer grasp their meaning. Were the under-nourished and imperiled poor of the world able to organize they could demand jobs, just wages, and a more equal distribution of land; but should a Moses figure emerge, his efforts would evoke accusations of a communist conspiracy.

Too many times in our own land we put in places of power those who aid and abet the oppression we claim to abhor. We return to office the rulers who have no sense of a "family of nations" and will take no risk for the common good. Instead, like Pharaoh, they have as their primary goal keeping the empire's riches and power in the hands of a few. A nation that claims to be in the Judeo-Christian tradition acts as though it had never read the story of Moses and Pharaoh, never heard the imperative of Jesus who said early in his life that he had come to preach good news to the poor, to proclaim release to the captives, and set at liberty the oppressed. As long as the gospel is announced apart from the present historical and social context, the truth of it will be lost. Only in an occasional church is justice being related to faith. We are not told that surrendering one's life to Jesus means becoming shepherds for the homeless, advocates for the poor, proclaimers of human rights, and creators of new liberating structures. Our Sunday schools are not teaching that the Red Sea crossing was a political event until Moses reflected on it from the viewpoint of the poor and interpreted it as God's intervention on behalf of Hebrew slaves. We are given very little help in identifying with the poor of our own cities and the poor of the world.

In Washington, D.C., illegal aliens, afraid to organize and too frightened to complain, are employed at miserable wages. They live eight and ten to a room in buildings along the streets I walk every day. When they fall ill they refuse to go to hospitals for fear of being deported. Those driven by fear and famine into our own Fertile Crescent area of the world are not, however, the only poor in the United States. We have our own native poor. They are hidden away in mountain towns, on farms and city streets. One day this summer at eleven in the morning I drove my car across Florida Avenue to U Street and on to 13th Street. I looked out on one of the saddest sights I have seen in Washington. Youth and able-bodied men were standing despondently in small groups on street corners where day laborers are recruited. These were the men not chosen. I was no longer perplexed by the story of Jesus' hiring a similar group late in the day and paying them a full day's wages. I have not made so sobering a journey since I drove in the midst of the teeming poor of India along the road that goes from New Delhi to the city of Agra where the Taj Mahal stands. But there was something more alive about the poor of India. They were engaged. They were at work, even though that work was collecting the dung of the cows and pounding it into cakes that could be burned to keep fires alive and water boiling.

The heaviness in my own spirit as I drove along our ghetto streets was induced by the sadness of the people I saw who have absorbed in their deepest beings the message that they are inferior. Though we live in a psychological age we have no understanding of the depression that grips our inner cities. Or could it be that too many of us are accomplices in their depression, preferring to keep the poor feeling guilty rather than to risk their rage?

The Church of The Saviour in Washington, D.C., has a mission group called Jubilee Jobs which came into being to find work for the so-called "hard-core unemployed," who are either unable to find work or unable to keep the jobs they do find. The counselors at Jubilee give encouragement to workers and employers alike, assuring them of help if they encounter difficulty. They call up employers to find out how new placements are doing, and they keep in touch with the new recruits so that those who start out scared to death, ready to panic in the face of any sign of rejection, can have the support they need to fight the urge to walk away when things are not going well.

Fear of failure is the reason so many of the poor do not get up in the morning. They have no confidence in their own ability to do what may be asked of them that day. Many have come to scorn themselves as well as to fear the scorn of others. They believe that they have nothing to give and that their terrible secret will be made known. Something in us perishes if we are not able to find and do the work connected with our deepest beings, but if we do not work at all the very self is lost.

I have digressed, however, from the Hebrews living in Egypt under the oppressive regime of the Pharaoh of Exodus. Can one push too far to find in their story a parallel with modern history? Can their struggles be similar to our own, separated as we are by more than three millennia?

The story in Exodus goes on to say that the Egyptians were motivated by no less an issue than population explosion. The crude method of birth control they devised was an order for the Hebrew midwives to kill all Jewish male babies. In an article[4] published over ten years ago Wilfried Daim stressed the more dominant fear that among those babies might be the leader of the revolution. We have seen that same fear in Herod and we are watching it today in the heart of white South Africa whose oppressive and fearful government is attempting to silence, imprison, kill, or send into exile any possible leader of the revolution. In Nicaragua last week a reporter asked a peasant woman, "But why do they kill the children?" The woman answered, "Because they are the seeds from which the subversives shall grow."

I drew closer to an understanding of Pharaoh when a friend pointed out to me that the population growth for whites in the United States has decreased dramatically while poor blacks and Hispanics are having babies in increasing numbers. The ranks of the poor have been further increased in our cities by Vietnamese, Haitians, Cambodians, and Ethiopians. I have rejoiced in the multicultural, multiracial face of America. I love the neighborhood in which I live. A ride on the bus up Columbia Road is like having a seat at the United Nations, but is it true that *my* number is decreasing and that *theirs* is increasing?

Long ago blacks in Washington, D.C., began to outnumber whites. Today they are 70 percent of the city's population. What if among them is a woman who bears the leader of the revolution—a Son of Man who will hear the cries of the people up and down U Street, the people crowded into vermin-infested rooms, and those sleeping on grates and in cardboard boxes? I already am careful to bar my door against the brutalized poor of the inner city. The criminals, however, are not the only ones with guns. The rich have far more. First they had them for hunting. Now they keep them close at hand—under beds, in bureau drawers, and on closet shelves. We have become a nation not only prepared for the coming of the Russians, but a nation armed against itself. In our streets are the sounds and marks of guerrilla warfare.

In ancient Egypt the Jews had no guns, but they had a hunger for things to be different, and that hunger can become a dreaded force. Those in power do well to fear the hunger of the people. Pharaoh moved decisively to cut off any future organized rebellion among the oppressed. He planned his strategy, however, without taking into account a few women who had nurtured caring in themselves. The Hebrew midwives became the leaders of the first resistance movement by refusing to carry out the Pharaoh's orders to kill. They make me wonder about the times in which I live and what is required of me.

Today here and there in our land a voice is raised urging us to refuse to pay our taxes that will be used for the building of a nuclear arsenal. Most people say they feel quite certain that one day nuclear warfare by intention or mistake will destroy the human race, and make the planet uninhabitable. Is this the time to reflect on the midwives of Egypt—those gentle and ordinary folk who found in themselves the will to defy a powerful despot? Of those women it was written, "since the midwives reverenced God he granted them descendants" (Exod. 1:21). I am reminded of those words as some eighteen-year-olds fail to register for the draft. Do not their elders need to encourage them in faithfulness to their vision of a peaceful kingdom, or have we become too schooled in obedience to kings? Herod also sent out his order to kill male babies because among them might be one who would be the leader of the revolution. He gave his order to the military and they were quick to comply. They had been tutored in death. The work the midwives did nurtured soul. As soon as a Hebrew woman became pregnant she chose her midwife. By the time of birth the bonds between the two women had been forged.

Are we not the midwives of the future? The Jewish scholar Arthur Waskow states what we all know, "It is our obligation to pass on to the next generation air that can be breathed, land that can bear fruit, water that can sustain life, the poetry and music of the ages. It is our obligation to pass on all that is in our genes." The question is, what is the work that will enable us to resist the architects of destruction so that it will be written of us, "They reverenced God and they were granted descendants"?

The fears of the Egyptian Pharaoh and of Herod were not groundless, nor are the fears of the privileged groundless today. When the gulf between rich people and poor people, between rich nations and poor nations grows too wide, the smoldering discontent is easily fanned. Among the Hebrews was a woman who bore the leader of the revolution. When the desperate Pharaoh sent out his order to throw into the river all the boy babies born to Hebrew mothers, she not only kept her son safe, but passed on to him her ingenuity and resourcefulness.

The gifted Levite boy grew up in Pharaoh's household, a foster child of wealth, educated with the Pharaoh's children. In the palace, he acquired a trained and disciplined intellect, as well as an insider's understanding of the workings of power. Jon Gunnemann states that "It is no accident that the leaders of a revolution are almost always renegades from the ruling class: it is they who understand power and are best equipped, having rejected an old paradigm, to engage in innovative reconstruction."

Reflecting on Moses with a clinician's insight, Wilfried Daim writes:

> Revolutionaries who are themselves in some sense members of the ruling classes typically solve their personal problems by identifying themselves with the lower classes. Marx and Engels, members of the bourgeoisie, identified themselves with the proletariat. Mao Tse-tung's father was a substantial farmer and rice merchant who, it now appears, treated his son with contempt, as though he was one of the servants. Mao became the peasants' revolutionary. He opposed his father by opposing the whole class to which his father belonged. All such revolutionaries, when struggling for the equality of the oppressed, fight for their own equality. And they oppose an entire social system in order to establish a new system that will not repeat the injustices of the old.

Daim speculates on what it must have been like for an "intruder from below" to grow up under Pharaoh's nose. He says that we can easily imagine how a palace teacher would treat a pupil who was more intelligent than the Pharaoh's own sons. "The teacher was bound to falsify, by lowering, his pupil's grades, thus preserving the belief that intelligence was a hereditary endowment in the royal blood."[5] Though we may know very little about what went on in Pharaoh's house, we do know that the small stranger who grew up there was lacking in self-confidence. He also was an angry young man and an adult stutterer. These were the overt signs of his distress.

Finally came that decisive day when Moses put aside caution about what others would think and set out to mingle with his countrymen. While he was observing how hard life was for them, an Egyptian struck a Hebrew. The rage in Moses, too long contained, erupted. Looking around and seeing no other overseer in sight, he killed the man and hid his body in the sand.

The next day he was drawn back to the scene of his crime. Despite the trouble he was in, his acute sensitivity to injustice led him to interfere again, this time in a dispute between two Hebrews. According to the biblical narrative he confronted the one who was in the wrong, "What do you mean by hitting your fellow countryman?" The man hurled back, "And who appointed you . . . to be prince over us, and judge? Do you intend to kill me as you killed the Egyptian?" (Exod. 2:14). Moses was alerted. He knew that what he had done was being talked about and that when the Pharaoh heard of the matter he would be killed. He had no alternative but to flee the land of his birth and become a political refugee.

Though Moses had lost home and position, the oppressed people he tried to serve felt no gratitude, a response that is not at all uncommon. Truly afflicted people do not seek deliverance from oppression. The prisoner of Chillon spoke for those in bondage when he said,

My very chains and I grew friends
So much a long communion tends
To make us what we are: even I
Regained my freedom with a sigh.[6]

As for those of us who would like some words of appreciation for trying to make things more fair, Paulo Freire instructs us well when he tells us that we have no right to expect gratitude for giving to another what is that other's due. Justice is a right and is always in everyone's interest. We are so wondrously made that when it is withheld, even when we are children, we know rage in our beings. If that rage cannot be expressed or used to set things right, it turns into hatred for the benefactor as well as for the oppressor. Moses did well to flee his country.

Having escaped to Midian, he rested one day by a well and watched as the daughters of the priest of Midian were driven away by a gang of shepherds who wanted the water for their own flocks. Moses in his characteristic way came to the rescue of the wronged, driving off the herdsmen and then helping the young women with the watering of their flock. When they went home and told the story to their father he sent for Moses, invited him to supper and then to stay on in his house. The pages of Exodus clearly indicate that the father came to love the young refugee. Perhaps he found in him the companion for whom his own questing mind and spirit yearned. In any case, from the beginning he sensed in Moses no ordinary person. He opened his house to him, gave him his flocks to look after and his daughter Zipporah in marriage.

In the next years Moses grew in his understanding of self and in his awareness of a larger world beyond the self. The signs of that growth are already evident at the birth of his first child. He named him Gershom, "because," he said, "I am a stranger in a foreign land" (Exod. 2:22). Moses knew the homesickness of the refugee. He knew also what it was to be taken in, cared for, and loved. He would never forget the mercy extended to him.

Protection for the stranger would be built into the laws of the new society that he was beginning to see with his mind's eye. As educator and legislator he would in the years to come repeat over and over again, "You must not oppress the stranger; you know how a stranger feels, for you lived as strangers in the land of Egypt" (Exod. 23:9). This same care for the stranger marked America's beginnings. A welcome to strangers, poor and huddled masses though they might be, was carved into the pedestal of the Statue of Liberty, lest the young nation of immigrants forget its origins. Today that reminder is most faithfully heeded in the Sanctuary Movement of the churches, giving shelter to refugees in danger of being hounded out of existence.

I was reminded of Moses and the boy called Gershom and the Statue of Liberty while walking through the refugee camps along the Thailand/Cambodian border. The people in the camps had the names of American cities on their lips and a light in their eyes when they spoke those names. I have never prayed more for my country than when walking among the refugees of Southeast Asia:

> America! America! God shed his grace on thee,
> And crown thy good with brotherhood
> From sea to shining sea! . . .
> America! America! God mend thine every flaw,
> Confirm thy soul in self-control,
> Thy liberty in law![7]

The Exodus narrative of freedom goes on to say,

> And the people of Israel groaned under their bondage and cried out for help, and their cry under bondage came up to God. And God heard their groaning, and God remembered his covenant . . . (Exod. 2:23–24, RSV).

The long imprisoned grief of the oppressed Hebrews broke forth in their cries, preparing them, as our cries prepare us, to know Yahweh's healing, liberating presence. Here the story of a people shifts back again to the "single one," to Moses, for God needs his *Other One*, a title borrowed from Nicholai Berdyaev. Yahweh heard the cries of the Israelites, but who will hear Yahweh's cry, "Whom shall I send, and who will go for us?" (Isa. 6:8, RSV).

The hard experiences in Moses' life opened him to an encounter with the God of the burning bush, but suffering alone does not make us co-creators with God, and co-creation is the essence of our vocation. While suffering has the possibility of awakening us to the divinity in ourselves, it has on the other hand the possibility of narrowing further our little worlds, making us bitter and resentful, quick to anger and to judge. Moses had the large work, as we all do, of engagement with dark forces churning within himself. He had to "seize the fire" (Blake) from the raging inferno in his own life, or there would be no burning bush, nor energy for the staggering task that was his destiny.

By imagination and empathy we can feel the drivenness of the young Moses, who swept down the Palace steps, past the gates of privilege to seek out the people who were his kin. In all likelihood it was an impulsive effort to assuage the untamed pain in himself. The short journey, however, was a fateful one, making him an exile and branding on his heart forever the grievous images of slavery. If in the country of his banishment Moses had been able to lose himself in activity and new friendships, he might have succeeded in putting the images of oppression behind him and escaped their life-changing impact. He was assigned, however, the solitary work of watching sheep— an occupation that gave him long hours to brood on his own history and touch new depths of despair in himself. In the silence Moses heard his own cries go up to God, heard them mingle with the cries of an afflicted people. Once more the pain in him had connected with the pain out there. "What must be done? What must I do? . . ."

Of one thing we can be certain. Vision does not come without contemplation. The silence formed Moses and informed him. The silence led him deeper into himself, on to that ground where no thoughts are, where no other creature may go, where the expectant soul attentively waits.

"Take off your shoes, for the place on which you stand is holy ground" (Exod. 3:5).

The I-Thou dialogue had begun, "Moses, you are not the only one to hear their cries. I, too, am well aware of their sufferings." Moses was then given the vocation to freedom that was his, and is everyone's. ". . . so come, I send you to Pharaoh" (Exod. 3:10).

The narrative says that the conversation took place at "the far side of the wilderness," where a man might wrestle with the implications of such an announcement. A thousand times Moses must have turned over in his mind the idea of a confrontation with Pharaoh and always drawn back, his heart ambivalent, his frame fraught with resistance. Now only one burning question remained to be put into words, "Who am I to go to Pharaoh?" (Exod. 3:11).

The reply made to Moses is the one given to every person seriously considering a human vocation toward a promised land of justice and caring: "I shall be with you . . ." (Exod. 3:11). One of the ways we know the call to be God's call is when a feeling of awe-filled dread is combined with one of being companioned.

. . . "and his name shall be called Emmanuel" (which means, God with us) (Matt. 1:23, RSV).

4

Being Present to the Moment

Last night was the first session in the class I am teaching "On Keeping a Journal." We used an exercise of Ira Progoff's, reflecting on every aspect of the preceding twenty-four hours, giving special attention to feelings we had experienced as we moved through the day. I like this exercise. It seems infinitely valuable. I always make the discovery of how full my day is but, more than this, that particular day becomes a more permanent part of my life. It is not what happens to us in any day that gives content to our lives, but whether or not we let its experience sink into us. As Moses learned, reflection is essential to that process. It is one of the highest powers given to anyone. In reflection I come upon feelings that I had been too afraid to experience in the moment. In the quiet of reflection I take the risk and the time to let censored thoughts as well as feelings into consciousness, to discover what is causing the uneasiness in me.

I continue to ponder Maurice Nicoll's observation that a day in one's life is a small replica of one's life:

> If a man does not work on a day in his life he cannot change his life, and if he says that he wishes to work on his life and change it, and does not work on a day in his life, his work on himself remains purely imaginary.[8]

Except for special events or unusual occurrences, most of our days have, as he says, a recurring similarity. If we want to change them we have to change our response to events in the day. A major discovery for me was how much of my life is spent in sheer maintenance—sleeping, washing, dressing, shopping, taking clothes to washers and dry cleaners, preparing meals, keeping records, writing checks, visiting dentists, doctors, garages, and inspection centers, getting haircuts, filling out tax returns, and making lists of things still to do—all those customary tasks that each one of us does, and that I am always hurrying through in order to do something I can call "important," as though any of us can know in advance what that might be. Thus I keep on hurrying through my life until there grows stronger in me the understanding that my redemption lies in my learning to love the commonplace.

"Meet the world," wrote Martin Buber, "with the fullness of your being and you shall meet him. That he himself accepts from your hands what you have to give to the world is his mercy. If you wish to believe, love!"[9]

Ann Lee, the founder of the Shaker community, gave these instructions: "Do all your work as if you had a thousand years to live, and as you would if you knew you must die tomorrow."[10] Her followers heeded those words and were responsible for the serenely beautiful Shaker-style furniture—one of the most admired of all design developments.

A legend about St. Francis tells that he was hoeing his garden one afternoon when someone asked him to speculate on what he would do if he knew he was going to die that day. "I would hoe my garden," he replied.

When I am faced with my death I would like to be so present to the task at hand that I would want to keep on with whatever happened to be my particular hoeing. To love is to be content with the present moment, open to its meaning, entering into its mystery.

5

On Praise

Every now and then I have a singing day. For no apparent reason I walk on winged feet, giving praise for the wonder of life and praise for the gratitude that so unexpectedly fills my being. In my mouth the poet's words: "Oh world, I cannot hold you close enough!"[11]

In contrast to those days are others with a special kind of anguish. They are the days when I feel solitary, cut off from the mainstream, misunderstood, and betrayed. I become the outsider, standing on the edges crying, "Look at me. I have something worth saying. I want to be listened to, I want to count, to be wanted and needed," crying my pain into hollow places that echo back those cries.

Is this God at work tearing down those things that have made me feel self-sufficient, helping me to move toward the experience of nothingness of which the saints write, the meaning of which is so hard to grasp? When we say that we are his, does he take us at our word, strip us of what has meaning—the friend we counted on, the work that seemed worthy enough to fill our days? Is it he who sets our feet upon that search within to find out why life has taken us into desert places? Is it he who forces us to look at all the corrosion that will not go away except in the heat of his fire? The saints would reply, "Yes. That is why we wrote all those pages on the dark night of the soul, that no one would be taken by surprise."

The bitter taste comes in the darkness when one hardly feels singled out for holiness. Any feeling of God has gone away. One is without comfort. If there be any constant companion it is the devil stalking to and fro, asking, "What have you got now? If this is Christian community, who wants it? You saved others, now save yourself. Obviously there is no one else around to do it."

These are the precise times to give praise—praise for the tempter's voice, praise for the pain, praise for sleepless nights and the agony of pounded or drenched pillows. Not praise for an exercise that will work good things for us, but praise to strengthen in ourselves faith in the resurrection, faith in the new being that is coming to birth in us, and the new world coming to birth out there, and the new heaven to come. Praise for the faith that our mourning, and crying, and pain make possible the new!

In my office hangs a little wooden plaque into which I have burned the words of Rabbi Moshe Hakotun:

> The praises
> of the sick
> and the
> broken
> excuse the
> silence of
> the healthy
> and
> whole.

6

On Money

The Ministry of Money held one of its many conferences on money this weekend. The group was made up of directors of foundations, church leaders, and businessmen, together with a few members of The Church of The Saviour. We had one day of silent retreat. The rest of the time we talked about money. We were a varied group ranging all the way from those who had great wealth to those who, having divested themselves of all possessions, were living austere lives or were members of communities that practiced the sharing of economic resources. Everyone had questions, some many more than others. A few of the affluent felt at ease with their wealth; some felt guilty; others had ambivalent feelings. Those with more modest incomes, however, had the same range of responses. How much money one has does not seem to determine how any of us relate to it.

I identified most with those who confessed their dread of poverty and their trust in money as a means of making life easier than it otherwise might be. They had an openness and willingness to search their pasts for hints and clues of how things were back then—of how parents and experiences might have shaped the choices they had made. Searching for a resolution of my own conflicts, I heard in their words the voices of fellow seekers. As the missions of the church give us more and more opportunities for direct contact with the poor, it is harder to go home to air-conditioned apartments and houses set in suburban woods. How much one should keep for oneself is no longer clear. Even the cost of educating our children, which we were once so assured we owed them, widens the gap between the poor and the rich—those who are beggars in the world and those who are givers.

The sharing of wealth has always made a lot of sense despite all the complicated feelings and circumstances that make it so incredibly difficult. The fact that the lives of Dorothy Day and Mother Teresa have a tremendous attraction for me made me wonder why I found so little inspiration in their counterparts at the Conference. Instead, I felt judged, even condemned by them. We shared a common vision of a just world, but no vital energy flowed from them to me to set ablaze a bush along my own path. I felt myself withdrawing from them. Could the reason be that these prophets at hand, delivering their message in person, were more threatening? I remembered a woman that I met in the coffee house of The Church of The Saviour. She told me that when she was living a thousand miles away she yearned for The Church of The Saviour to be in her hometown. Nine months ago she had moved to Washington, D.C., and this was her first visit. She had not planned to speak to anyone. When I asked "Why?" she simply said that she was afraid of the commitment the church asked. "I am not ready to make that kind of commitment." Both of us reminded me of the rich young ruler—attracted by what we heard, but unable to relinquish our hold on what we had.

Perhaps, however, those rich young folk living on minimum incomes disturbed me most because I harbor the suspicion that I sometimes sound like them, even though I am not at their place of commitment. I have grave doubts that my own standard of living is in keeping with what I glimpse of the world that is straining to be born, and from time to time I find myself wanting to make my friends feel equally ill at ease with their comfortable lifestyles. The vague assumption is that with this accomplished we might together muster the courage to make more radical changes in our lives. We might become poor but no one would be lonely. More than we realize, or would like to admit, we rely on money to give us companionship and to protect us from the threat of isolation.

A materialistic, consumer society arises out of a feeling of emptiness inside—an inner poverty that feeds our fear. Greed is actually a symptom of spiritual starvation—the lack of meaningful relationships and meaningful work. We have always known that the lack of a nurturing mother or mother substitute in the early years is crippling to a child's development. Now we must ask if the lack of appropriate work in the adult years does not impair and debase the developing self. I know that when I am doing a "good work" I grow rich inside, more responsible, willing to sacrifice.

Thinking about it all, especially my own dependence on money, I want to acknowledge aloud all those dark, unacceptable strands that weave in and out of my life, so that the whole of me can be baptized into the new. This means I cannot be an idealized mother, or sister, or church leader. There is no liberation for anyone in that role. Better that we all be pilgrims together, helping each other to discover the path that is our path—never discerned without hard work. I have sometimes wondered if reformers do not sound harsh and self-righteous because they have not listened to tremblings and beckonings within. Have they ruthlessly cut down the wheat of their life along with the chaff? Perhaps it is inner division, or vague regrets, or unlived life, or envy of the rich that gives to any voice a judgmental note.

I am convinced that every human who treads this earth— rich and poor and in-between—is destined to join the liberation movement that is going on all over the world. For any full involvement, however, each of us must struggle for agreement between all those disparate selves who live in us—especially with that self who is the guardian of our economic interests. If our struggling inner selves can come to a summit meeting and agree to set out to create the new order throbbing in the world and at our own center, it will not matter so much how many around us we persuade to come along. If need be, we will be able to take leave of old friends, confident that we have, or will be given, whatever is needed to sustain us on the journey.

7

On Dialogue

Dialogue is more than your giving me space to say my words, and my giving you space to say yours. It involves our listening. We are all very different. We cannot have dialogue unless we honor the differences. How can I build a bridge across the gulf between me and you unless I am aware of the gulf? How can I communicate with you unless I see how things look from your side?

Dialogue demands that I leave the place where I dwell—the

landscape of feelings and thoughts that are important to me—in order to dwell for a time with your thoughts, feelings, perceptions, fears, hopes. I must deny myself—forsake the familiar, give up my life—in order to experience your life.

The purpose of dialogue is never to persuade another person to accept our opinions, or values, or view of the world; rather it is to create understanding—a climate where communion takes place. He who has lost himself finds himself. The deepest craving of every heart is to be laid bare, to be known, to be understood. The imperative statement, "Come and see a man who has told me everything I ever did," will always give rise to the thought, "I wonder if he is the Christ?" (John 4:29).

If ever we take the time to know another life, we will be experienced as godly—as "one who cares." When we are listened to and understood, the clouds roll back, the dawn breaks, Christ comes.

But how many of us can take time to understand, or even time to make ourselves understood? There is always some place to go, or something to do, secrets to protect.

And if we do not take time to understand each other, how can we take time to understand God?

> The ox knows its owner
> and the ass its master's crib,
> Israel knows nothing,
> my people understands nothing.
> Isaiah 1:3

8

The Child's Wisdom

I had lunch today with Sherry Stryker, whose training is in anthropology and linguistics. She has taught English as a second language for many years and developed her own program of teaching. I told her that our mission group working with refugees was exploring the addition of an English program for homebound refugees, and she immediately offered to help train teachers. Having lived for a great many years in Eastern Asia, she remembers the cultural shock and loneliness of her first years in a country not her own, and has a deep empathy for the refugees who are trying to start all over again in America.

I shared with her how enthralled I was with the children of Vietnam, Laos, and Cambodia whom I first met in the refugee camps of Thailand. Sherry said that most Asian children seem to be rushing toward life. As a young mother living in China, she had carefully observed the children of Southeast Asia and attributes their very special vitality to the way they are raised. She finds it incredible that this country with its deep concern for children has no published study on how the Chinese raise their children.

In China, Sherry said, "the assumption is that every person is born good. The baby as well as the child is considered to have all the wisdom of an adult. The baby innately knows what it needs. It is unthinkable in that country that an adult would not meet its needs—not feed the baby when it is hungry, or pick it up when it cries. The baby goes everywhere the mother goes. It is held in a sling close to the mother's body rather than in a plastic container on an aluminum frame where it cannot hear the mother's beating heart and feel the warmth of her body. Children have an immense need for closeness. It gives them the feeling of being loved and of self-worth."

In China there are no "terrible twos." What the child wants, you give to it. Its autonomy is respected. There is pleasure in the infant's testing of itself in the larger world, delight in the toddler's adventuring on its own, and delight in its return. One never sees a healthy adult pushing a child away. This all changes when the child is three. The child is then expected to behave in an adult way, but this is what the three-year-old wants to do anyway. At three the child's delight is in imitating adults. By the time Asian children are on their own, they have developed inner resources that stand them in good stead all of their lives.

I liked listening to Sherry. I too feel that the child is full of wisdom. All this summer I have so often been amazed at the Asian child who frequently stays with me. With almost too much life to be contained in one five-year frame, she has at the same time an easy obedience, even when it comes to going to bed. It is as though she trusts that the instructions I give are in her interest. At the same time she has no conviction of my infallibility. Sometimes she will ask, "How did you know that?" and I will teasingly reply, "I know everything." "Oh, no you don't," she will come back. "Remember last night you didn't know where your keys were. Remember yesterday when . . . ."

This child and I had two rare conflicts of will in the month of August. All six pairs of her new socks had disappeared. When I sent her home with clothes she usually failed to return with them. Perhaps they went to other children or perhaps they were simply lost amidst the belongings of many adults trying to share one tiny apartment. In any case on a hot August day her sole possession was one pair of heavy knee-high socks, which she insisted on wearing. I said no and she said yes. Sitting on the edge of her bed I decided to explain myself more fully. "Helen," I said, "the reason I don't want you to wear these socks is that today is going to be a very hot day, and you will be uncomfortable." I even threw in an explanation of how often sandals were worn without socks. Having made this appeal to reason, I confidently told her the choice was hers. She looked at me soberly with those "five-summer eyes" and said, "I will wear them." I was surprised at my irritation with the decision. I had not known how much I wanted my will to prevail.

On the way to school she sat silently beside me and folded the bulky socks down to ankle length, while I reflected on how blistered her little feet had been several weeks before. Perhaps she had also recalled her painful feet and decided that it was better to be hot and to risk my displeasure than to have feet that hurt.

"You know," I confided, "I think you made a good choice about the socks." The enchanting child looked up with pure delight in her face. Whatever reasoning lay behind her choice of socks it was absolutely clear that to wear them was of utmost importance. She was relieved to know that at last I approved of what she was unable to explain.

The second revolt came again over clothes. She had so few and most of them consisted of shorts she refused to wear. Finally with embarrassment she explained that they made her look like a boy. No amount of assurance persuaded her otherwise. Weeks later I learned from her mother that the children in her neighborhood had, indeed, thought she was a boy, and had teased her when she insisted that she was a girl. Her deeply offended self could not bear to have that happen again. What did all the assurance of adults matter? Experience had taught her that the facts were otherwise. I could wait for her to learn that her playmates were not the whole world. I was surprised at how quickly she was to make that discovery.

This small Buddha girl has also taught me to move more slowly. When she is with me I allow twice as long for everything, a practice I so badly need. She who loves to race, also loves to take time to see how keys fit into locks, to amble on the stairs, to study the odd assortment of objects in the universe, and especially to contemplate the children on the street. She also enjoys reflecting on her day and sometimes on her life. When the bedtime story has been read, she likes time to ask, "Do you remember when we went to the store . . . ? Do you remember . . . ?"

I who try to practice and to teach reflection sometimes have to battle hard not to impose on her a rhythm not her own. I learn from her to deal with my own hurrying toward the next moment and to surrender to the intimate sharing that she offers me in this one.

The hunger for closeness seems so acute in the world. Many times we may blunder right by it when it is being offered, creating in ourselves an emptiness and passing on to our children a faulted way of being in the world.

9

On Bravery

This evening as I stopped my car for a red light on Columbia Road an old woman, deformed by age, caught my attention. In one hand she grasped a four-pronged, aluminum walking cane, and, in the other, a fishnet shopping bag. Every step seemed a painful effort. It would be a long time—maybe half an hour—before she reached the supermarket in the middle of the block. Her path was impeded by construction work, street vendors, darting children, a homeless man, and other shoppers. Across the street in front of the Ontario Theater the drug dealers were making sales. Her frailty made the whole street seem dangerous and reminded me of the bag snatchings in that area and of how often the old are the victims.

Long after I had moved on, the woman stayed in my thoughts. She still does. I have wondered where she lives, how much her survival depended on her journey and whether, although there may have been someone else to make the trip, she had chosen to go herself. Mostly I have wanted to be instructed by her courage. I have wished the wind could take to her my thoughts.

Thank you, old woman, for modeling independence in the midst of ravaged years. I want your image stored away in me for protection against the fear of my own aging. You are more help than the extra hospital plan or the savings account. I will draw upon you to send scurrying the ghosts of timid ones guarding themselves against drafts, over-exertion, and attacks from thieves and germs. When I am tempted to join their frightened company, or to let others wait on me, or to hoard my life, I want to remember you and the menacing look of that street, and how you so gallantly set forth.

10

On Growing Old

I saw the old woman again today. We both live in the neighborhood of The Potter's House, which is a European-type coffeehouse and bookstore, operated by The Church of The Saviour since 1960. The five-year-old with me, so good at mimicking, imitated the bent stance and the faltering steps. Her eight-year-old companion reproached her gently with only a hint of rebuke in her tone. "You will be old like that one day, and you will die, too." Her mother, Janelle Goetcheus, the doctor at the health clinic on the corner, has educated her daughter's heart in these matters.

The five-year-old asks, "Why doesn't she die?"

"Because," says her grave mentor, "God is not ready for her. He wants her to be here."

The children fell silent, perhaps considering the information so matter-of-factly given. They may have been reflecting as I was on God's wanting her to be here. To me the news seemed fresh and unclaimed.

Tonight I hunted up an interview with Ken Kesey in which he described his experience on the geriatric wards of a Veteran's Administration Hospital. The compassionate Kesey is no sentimentalist. He tells things as they are:

> These wards are concrete barns built, not for attempted treatment of the herds of terminal humanity that would otherwise be roaming the streets, pissing and drooling and disgusting the healthy citizenry, but for nothing more than shelter and sustenance, waiting rooms where old guys spend ten, twenty, sometimes thirty years waiting for their particular opening in the earth. At eight in the morning they are herded and wheeled into showers, then to Day Rooms where they are fed a toothless goo, then are plunked into sofas ripe with decades of daily malfunctions of worn-out sphincters, then fed again, and washed again, and their temperatures taken if they're still warm enough to register, and their impacted bowels dug free in the case of sphincters worn-out in the other direction, and their hair and cheesy old finger nails clipped (the clippings swept into a little pink and grey pile), and fed again and washed again, and then usually left alone through the long afternoons.[12]

Kesey writes about conditions that enrage my own heart. Only today, men not much better off than those he describes are released to the streets. They wander into the Columbia Road Health Service and turn Janelle's heart to dreaming of a center where she and other doctors can care for them. I want such a center also, but in me is a deep fear of it. Part of me, not so sure that we could create a more caring community for them, shrinks from so arduous a work. Kesey describes the response of the young attendants who care for the men that even the doctors called vegetables, as though the classification were permissible:

> . . . After the first meal squeezed into a slack mouth, or after the first diaper change or catheter taping, every one of the trainees has thought this thought, and some have spoken it: "Without our help these guys would die!"
> And, after the hundredth feeding and diapering and changing,

the next thought, though never spoken, is: "Why don't we just let them die?"

An awful question to find in your head, because even young aides know that age can happen to anyone. "This could I someday be." But even fear of one's own future can't stop the asking: Why don't we just let them die? What's wrong with letting nature take its own corpse? Why do humans feel they have the right to forestall the inevitable fate of others?[13]

It was Freddy Schrimpler who helped Kesey find a satisfying answer to his question. Freddy was seventy-eight or eighty. He had been on the geriatric ward for close to twenty years. All that time he did nothing but lie on his side under a sheet. The only sound he made was a muffled squeaking back in his throat. Kesey discovered that he could speak. Bit by bit he learned Freddy's story.

A stroke years ago had suddenly clipped all the wires leading from the brain to the body. He found that while he could hear and see perfectly, he couldn't send anything back out to the visitors that dropped by his hospital bed more and more infrequently. Finally they sent him to the VA, to this ward where, after years of effort, he had learned to make his little squeak. Sure, the doctors and nurses knew he could talk, but they were too busy to shoot the breeze and didn't really think he should exhaust himself by speaking. So he was left on his gurney to drift alone in his rudderless vessel with his shortwave unable to send. He wasn't crazy; in fact the only difference that I could see between Freddy and Buddha was in the incline of their lotus position. As I got to know him I spoke of the young aide's thought.

"Let a man die for his own good?" he squeaked, incredulous. "Never believe it. When a man . . . when anything . . . is ready to stop living . . . it stops. You watch . . ."

Before I left the ward, two of the vegetables died. They stopped eating and died, as though a decision of the whole being was reached and nothing man or medicine could do would turn this decision. As though the decision was cellularly unanimous . . .[14]

When I talk with friends about the possible years of our dying, most of us say that we do not want a "lingering" old age, as though we knew of some who would choose it. Anyone who has worked on a geriatric ward finds it almost impossible to imagine being a patient on such a ward. If Freddy Schrimpler was right, however, the fact that we live indicates, no matter what our circumstances, that somewhere in us is our free consent to live. Is he saying that, when the spirit fully gives up, the body complies with the decision? I am not as sure as he was. When I picture myself in some of the grim conditions under which people live I can imagine myself wanting to wrest from the body its claim on life. It is, nonetheless, an uneasy thought.

When we ponder these things we ponder not only darkness, but the mystery that lies at the heart of most serious questions. "Into thy hands I commit my life" seems in keeping with that mystery. I feel more peaceful when I can make that statement. Is this not what is meant by a life lived in surrender? The mystic's yes to all that is.

I look at myself and around me and see the different ways in which people age. Some have smooth necks but humps on their backs; some have straight backs but gnarled fingers; some who have agile, graceful bodies like young gazelles do not know what day it is. When we are still very young we can feel and see in ourselves the hints of our dying. Nature, too, instructs us. I think about this as I watch the leaves on the trees outside my windows. Some fall when they are still green; others go down in a brilliance of color; still others when they are withered; and then there is that last brown one that clings to a bare branch through the whole of winter.

Though I may wish to be the flaming leaf, only one thing is clear about my dying: I am not supposed to know the way it will be. Mine is simply to practice saying yes to life and yes to death and to whatever comes with one or the other. Each day the practice of surrender, each day the practice of letting go.

11

Letting Go

These many years I have been working with the theme
of "letting go." Every day, as well as every new stage of life,
offers opportunity for that work. To relinquish the people one
loves is especially hard, and yet this is the nature and requirement of love. While I cling to another, I can never truly love
that person. When I love the other I will free him or her to
follow a path that is not my path, to hold opinions that are in
opposition to my own, to have friends that will never be my
friends, to live in a city that is not my city, to leave the circle of
my love for another's love. Anne Lindbergh wrote:

> Him that I love, I wish to be
> Free—
> Even from me.[15]

"Let my people go," Moses cried out to Pharaoh, as life cries
out to us. When that demand is made upon my heart by those
who would walk away from me, I struggle for a strong yes, only
to discover that its very utterance causes me to fall into sorrow-
ful places. Bit by bit I take back the permission given. I do it by
tone, glance, or gesture, by the critical word or the artful question, or by encouragement withheld. Like the Pharaoh of Exodus I cry, "Yes, I have seen the sign of your God. You may go
free," and then I harden my heart and must be given a new
sign.

"Let my people go." How do we do that? I know of no other
way except to give one's blessing and to mean it. If we do not
mean it, it will have no healing power. Jacob needs the blessing
of the father if he is to leave the home of his childhood, and we
need the blessing of each other to be set free.

The parent who has blessed the child leaves that child free to

run toward life. The parent who has withheld his or her blessing binds the child in intractable ways. The blessing is integral
to the experiencing of our separateness—to being our own
persons and going our own ways.

The cry of Esau, "Father, bless me too!" (Gen. 27:34) springs
from the innermost core of our own hearts. We need to be
blessed, and the blessing must be genuine. Perhaps the stolen
blessing of Jacob proved worthless because it was secured by
fraud. He must wrestle with the angel because he needs a
blessing intended only for him. "I will not let you go unless you
bless me" (Gen. 32:26). It is not possible just to go our own way.
We need to be sent, "As the Father sent me, I send you," or we
look back with too much pain.

Perhaps those who clutch the most and who block our way
never felt blessed themselves. When a fearful Pharaoh finally
tells Moses and Aaron that they are free to worship Yahweh:
"Take your flocks and herds, and go," he adds a plaintive request, "And also ask a blessing on me" (Exod. 12:32).

To bless the people who have oppressed our spirits, emotionally deprived us, or in other ways handicapped us, is the most
extraordinary work any of us will ever do. Hate and bitterness
grow when we have to wrest ourselves from the control of another, or leave the household of our parents without feeling that
we were smiled upon.

Today a friend of mine recalled with sadness two bright
occasions from her childhood. One was as a very small child
when, hearing her father at the door, she hid under the table.
From that place she heard her father ask her mother, "Where
is Jenny?" She was ecstatic. She had not really expected him to
miss her and, when he did, she was filled with a wild kind of
joy. The second time was when her father took her, a teenager,
to a movie and introduced her to one of his friends as "my date
for the evening." Again, pure joy filled her being. She remembers these times with sadness as the only times when the god
who was her father got across to her that she mattered to him.
They were not enough to nurture the conviction in her that he

enjoyed being with her, and that she was, therefore, an enjoyable person. She is quite confident now that he really did love her, but this does not keep her from being angry with him, and from feeling that he is somehow responsible for the immense hole inside her, a pain that she does not know how to assuage.

I have a memory from childhood that is unlike hers, but holds the same message. My father was refusing to let my older sister go on a date unless she would be back at what to her seemed an unreasonably early hour. I heard caring in that discipline and hope sprang in me that, when I reached my sister's age, my father would care enough to notice when I went out and when I returned.

Yearning for the blessing never given can keep us forever fixed in the past, forever wanting what was withheld, forever looking to authority figures and significant others for the benediction a parent never gave. The situation is more grievous still when a parent not only fails to communicate love, but also transmits hostile feelings. Then not only does the past fail to bless us—it sends us limping into each new day.

Moses had the task of dealing with grievous wrongs. Uprooted from his home a second time and sent into exile, he could have turned to hating. He might have easily internalized the father of his Egyptian household and become a new and more terrible despot. This is, after all, the response of most revolutionaries who succeed in overthrowing the old. They do no inward work, and thus are compelled to repeat the model they swear they will never copy. They fail to let their hearts be informed by long stretches of silence. Moses, the liberator, was also a shepherd, a brooder, a listener to heavenly voices. He who was the son of slaves had also called a Pharaoh "father." Child of the oppressed, somewhere in his journey he must have yielded to the plea of the oppressor, "And also ask a blessing on me," and knelt to petition Yahweh to forgive the man who had wielded power so abusively. "Father, forgive him for he knows not what he does." Without that prayer Moses could never have spoken for Yahweh the third commandment,

"Honor your father and your mother," though one was a Pharaoh and the other an Egyptian princess.

Forgiveness is integral to letting go. We are bound to the people we cannot forgive. Holding even a small grudge takes up space in the soul and captures the energy needed for moving on. To bless the people who are our oppressors is the only way to heal the wounds they have inflicted and to break the chains that bind us to them.

Forgiveness is an essential dimension of letting go. Standing on one's own feet is another. They can be so interrelated that it is hard sometimes to know where one begins and the other ends. I cannot forgive someone on whom I am emotionally dependent. There is too much anger involved in a dependent relationship. By grace we have anger to help extricate ourselves from overly dependent stances in life.

Christianity says we are to share together a common life (John 1:7). We are to be so intimately bound that we are to experience ourselves as one body—a single new humanity. At the same time everyone is to know that before God she is alone. "You must work out your own salvation in fear and trembling . . ." (Phil. 2:12, NEB). After Paul has instructed us that we are to help each other in carrying the heavy burden of the life of transformation (Gal. 6:2), he reminds us that everyone is responsible for his own life (Gal. 6:5). We are to hold each other and to let each other go. These two teachings of Christianity are not as contradictory as they sound. Holding is what makes possible letting go and letting go, in its turn, makes possible holding.

We are to hold each other and to let each other go. One movement makes possible the other. Distance gives the space in which to reach out and hold. The intimacy of holding gives strength to the inner person—the nourishment that enables us to speed another on his way.

To stand on one's own two feet may be the real work of love. Since there is not an abundance of love in our world, none of us can assume that we have done that work well. If we realized the significance of that achievement, I believe we would pursue our independence with less embarrassment and more commitment. In his Asian journal, Thomas Merton tells a story about a young Tibetan lama who was faced with leaving his country. His land was being occupied by Chinese communists, and he and the other abbots were in grave jeopardy. While he was absent from his abbey, the situation grew even more grave. Uncertain as to what to do next, he sent a message to a nearby abbot friend asking, "What do we do?" His friend sent back an uncluttered response, "From now on, Brother, everybody stands on his own feet."

"To my mind," wrote Thomas Merton, "that is an extremely important monastic statement. If you forget everything else that has been said, I would suggest you remember this for the future: 'From now on, everybody stands on his own feet.' . . . You cannot rely on structures. The time for relying on structures has disappeared. They are good and they should help us, and we should do the best we can with them. But they may be taken away, and if everything is taken away, what do you do next?"[16]

In her collection of *Hasidic Tales of the Holocaust*, Yaffa Eliah records a similar message in "No Time for Advice." Rabbi Simcha, known as a scholar and wise man, advised his children, Moishe Dovid and Bluma, to flee to Warsaw as the safest place of refuge from the Germans. The road to that city was crowded and Moishe Dovid is separated from Bluma and never sees her again. Doubting that it was wise to have left his home he seeks the guidance of the Grand Rabbi Pabianic, who has always had the right word for every situation. He is shocked when the Rabbi responds, "Don't ask me any questions! This is no time for advice." Following his own intuition he returns home to a grateful father. He inquires of the father why the Grand Rabbi could give no counsel. In the father's answer are these words, "It is a time such as we have never experienced before. Each of us must make his own decisions, for each of us will ultimately be called to be a member of the Sanhedrin and sit in judgment in matters of life and death, to judge his own life. My son, the

Grand Rabbi of Pabianic was right. I was wrong and my dear beautiful daughter, Bluma, the flower of my life, has paid dearly, with her life, for my decisions and advice." Thereafter Moishe Dovid always made his own decisions and survived six years under German occupation.[17]

These stories have engraved themselves on my own memory because I have stood in such need of them. I have been slow to learn that my advice as well as the other's advice is always very subjective, determined by one's own experiences, special biases, self-interest, and blindness. Standing on one's own two feet is the equivalent of growing up. It means knowing that the answers to one's life lie deep in one's own being. It is believing that within one's own heart are the intuition and wisdom needed for choosing the way one is to go. It is holding the same belief for another. This does not mean I do not need to tell my story to another. In listening to my dilemma my friend helps me to sort through the chaff in my life so that I can uncover the truth that is mine—touch that oasis of health within myself that will let me be in the world as a whole person. Basic to that process are the understanding and acceptance of my aloneness. Without that understanding and acceptance I look to others for what they cannot give me. I think that if I did not have my child, or my friend, or my work, I would be alone and feel lonely, whereas we are alone even though we have all these and more. Though I may think it is peculiar to myself, loneliness is part of the human condition. To remind me of that and for sharing I carry this quote around in my wallet:

> According to the Teachers, there is only one thing that all people possess equally. This is their loneliness. No two people on the face of this earth are alike in any one thing except for their loneliness. This is the cause of our growing, but it is also the cause of our wars. Love, hate, greed and generosity are all rooted within our loneliness, within our desire to be needed and loved.[18]

If we could dare to face and accept the fact that we are alone, then we would know that every other person is also alone. It does not matter how surrounded the other is by friends and family. She, too, is alone. If we could know with certainty that well-guarded secret, perhaps we would move toward the other with more compassion, be less ready to judge, less quick to do those things which will cause the other to withdraw from us. Yet loneliness is the secret we keep from ourselves as well as from others. It is as though some shame were connected with it—if I am not loved, I must somehow be responsible for it.

It is when I grieve or suffer bodily pain that I am most apt to be confronted with my aloneness. No matter how much another cares, he goes away and leaves me with my tears and the long night. Though he promised me his thoughts, even they can be taken away by the most ordinary events.

Even when I receive news of the other's impending death, my thoughts are propelled toward life—away from the pain of letting go. I have felt in me a shameful preoccupation with filling the void that threatens to be there. The very interdependence of love makes the preservation of the self an issue in the beloved's death. Will I be able to stand when the other falls? What will I do with the empty spaces? Will the energy that went into our shared life be forever contained within me, coursing through my body as a wild, trapped pain?

Too often, rather than be abandoned, we abandon the dying, rush to take care of our panic before it is upon us, take the complete plunge into a separate existence to avoid its being thrust upon us, leave the beloved in order to prepare for his leaving of us. This can happen even when we are the ones who move toward partings less final than death. I remember when a friend of mine came to the Washington area from a midwestern state where his life was deeply invested in a neighborhood church community. After he made his decision to leave he felt himself growing critical of his friends, even angry with them. Only after he was rooted in his new surroundings was he able to look back and ask, "What was that all about?" and to know that it was his way of protecting himself from the pain of separation. "I was trying to tell myself, they are not important to me. I can get along without them."

Loneliness is part of our human lot while at the same time community remains a basic human need. I can never be sure of how much aloneness my particular human heart can bear. The pain of separation is intensified when it throws me back on old feelings of abandonment and rejection, for these are the fears that crop up in every leave-taking.

When we can fully recognize the reality of our aloneness, something happens in us which is tied in with letting go and becoming responsible for our own lives. The child becomes the parent, the pupil the teacher, the patient the healer, the disciple the redeemer. One discovers in one's self the power to bless and the power to forgive sins. This must be what Meister Eckhart meant when he said, "Our letting go is in order that God might be God in us."

12

Imaging Caring Institutions

Every time I visit Richard I find him waiting by the door as though he had been told I was coming. He is now in a small center for elderly and disabled men, but it was the same when he was on the back wards of mental institutions. He would spend his days in the long corridor peering through the small glass window in the locked door. The nurses on those wards would tell me that he had been asking whether this was the day his sister was coming. My sadness is that he is asking that question on all the days I do not come. No wonder, although my hours overbrim with more gifts than I can possibly use, I live my life in awareness of other worlds where the people one waits for do not come, and there is nothing to break the sameness of the days.

In his journals Emerson wrote:

> Now for near five years I have been indulged by the gracious Heaven in my long holiday in this goodly house of mine entertaining and entertained by so many worthy and gifted friends and all this time poor Nancy Barron the mad-woman has been screaming herself hoarse at the poorhouse across the brook and I still hear her whenever I open my window.[19]

Had I been Emerson, I would have moved. The window in my house that opens on such a scene is independent of geography. Looking through it I have caught a vision of Christ's new earth and have come to understand that it is every person's vocation to create that earth. We are to cast out demons, be healers, artists, musicians, the builders of caring institutions. Creativity is not the work of a few. We each carry within us the image of God the Creator; we each have the task of making the earth into a fairer, kinder place. The first step is imaging a better world, and that is most apt to happen when we suffer or look on suffering. The difficulty is that we do not take the next step of creating the world we envision. We lack the courage or somehow feel that this is someone else's responsibility rather than the work of the one who sees and images something different and higher.

We are not powerless in the oppressive situations in which we feel caught. We are not bound to the reality we see. We are creators. We can make the new.

When I return from the five-hundred-mile round-trip visit to see Richard, the longing to have him nearer is fresh in me again. I want to be about the search to find a "place" for him that is closer and generates life and spirit. If I fail in that search, I want to create such a place. None exists now in the Washington area. In the District of Columbia, patients considered well enough to be "main-streamed back into the community" (the current deceptive vernacular for the program in force) live in inadequate half-way houses which require of their occupants more self-sufficiency than Richard has. The only alternative is some miserable boardinghouse or the sidewalk.

The fact that between 50 and 70 percent of our "street people" are severely ill mental patients is now being freely acknowledged. The plight of the mentally ill who roamed her streets moved eighteenth-century England to establish the first asylum for their care. Today in our country only occasional groups attempt to meet the need, and their limited funds provide a place to sleep for only a very few. For the most part this lost and stricken segment of our citizenry goes unmentioned. Feature stories appear in newspapers from time to time, mostly initiated by local people who are either made uncomfortable by the peculiar population in their midst or are concerned about the effect on real estate values. The greatest sufferers, however, are not those in the hapless neighborhoods into which state hospitals are dumping their poor, but the mental patients themselves. They too often look out at us through eyes that register neither complaint for their plight, nor comprehension of the storms around them.

> Harshly dealt with, he bore it humbly,
> he never opened his mouth,
> like a lamb that is led to the slaughterhouse,
> like a sheep that is dumb before its shearers
> never opening its mouth.
>
> Isaiah 53:7

13

No Place

When Helen Cary and I traveled to Richmond today we were hopeful that we might find some suitable place there for Richard. The names on my list, however, turned out to be nursing facilities occupied by very old people lying in beds or sitting inert in wheelchairs. An occasional person would plead for our attention as we passed by. At each place we asked for and were given the name of an adult community home that might be worth checking out. The charges to residents in these centers were from $800 to $900 a month, half the cost of the "convalescent homes," but still beyond the means of most of the wounded and old. These, too, proved inadequate and depressing. People standing, people sitting. Everyone doing nothing. I thought of lines from a poem by Sara Teasdale lodged in memory from long ago:

> Hope went by and Peace went by
> And would not enter in;
> Youth went by and Health went by
> And Love that is their kin.
>
> Those within the house shed tears
> On their bitter bread;
> Some were old and some were mad,
> And some were sick a-bed.
>
> Gray Death saw the wretched house
> And even he passed by—
> "They have never lived," he said
> "They can wait to die."[20]

To give up hope for another human being is a terrible thing, no matter what the person's age or condition. Not only is it a cruel form of rejection, it allows us to justify not doing for another what otherwise might be done. I know that I would fold up and die inside if someone I cared about or someone on whom I depended were to give up hope in me—ceased to believe in my future, my capacity to change and to be new. Such abandonment usually coming at a time when a human being is most powerless, most dependent on mercy, destroys the very soul.

14

Who Hears Prayer?

Writing about the community homes reminded me of an evening when I was part of the volunteer staff of an overnight shelter for street women. It was a very cold night and the women began to arrive early in the evening. The rooms reserved for them were behind the sanctuary of the church and were used for other purposes during the day. Foam rubber mats were laid out over the entire area in one room. Many of the women chose a mat as soon as they arrived. Some had very little with them, though most of them had the bags that have given them the name of bag ladies. One carried her possessions in a child's wagon, and another, more affluent, had hers piled dangerously high in a supermarket cart. The conversation was disconnected, but the atmosphere was warm and peaceful. Each one was given a bowl of stew, bread, and tea.

While most of the women made their beds on a mat in the large room, others chose to sit up the whole night. A woman sitting close to me said aloud to anyone who might be listening, "Wouldn't it be nice if we did not have to leave in the morning?" Some women slept sitting up, but others rocked back and forth most of the night. The room had the look and feel of wards I have seen in large mental institutions. For the first time I knew beyond any doubt that many of these were not street people because they were poor, but because they were mentally ill. Unable to provide for themselves any permanent kind of home, they were sentenced, maybe forever, to wander aimlessly through a city that was without shame.

When morning came the peaceful atmosphere inside the shelter turned hostile. Distraught women—some of them old and sick—could not comprehend why they were once more being "pushed out" into the streets. We who had received them so warmly the night before were the very ones hurrying them along, benefactors so soon become enemies.

In the narrow hall where the women were having breakfast, an old woman with a gentle face kneeled to pray. She was in the way of another woman who taunted her, "Get up woman. God don't hear your prayer." The praying woman did not respond and her taunter said again, "God don't hear your prayer, woman. God don't hear your prayer."

I asked myself, "Does God hear her prayer?" Then I remembered. God is in me and where I am God is. The real question was, "Did I hear her prayer?" What would it mean to hear her prayer?

Scenes like that keep me asking what I must do to provide places for some of the homeless in our land—the mentally ill, the retarded, the old, the poor. They influence what I think and feel, and how I write and speak and teach. They keep me questing for my place in the building of a new society.

15

Being Old

I recounted for Gordon my survey of nursing homes. He told me about his mother-in-law, whom he and Mary had moved from a nursing facility in the Washington area to one in her hometown of Lynchburg, Virginia. Last night Gordon's brother, Bev, called to say that she had come out of her comatose state and wanted to visit a fountain that had been erected as a monument to their mother—her life-time friend. Gordon was convinced that her revived spirit was due to her many visitors. "All her life," he said, "she has thrived on company."

Joan Dodge has a story about her grandmother that I find equally instructive. Her grandmother, who was an active, alert woman of ninety-four, began to complain of not feeling well. She was taken several times to the doctor, and each time she complained to him that she was feeling dragged out and that she lacked her usual energy. Each time he checked her over and said words to the effect that, at her age, she should expect to have to slow down. Her grandmother still complained of increasing fatigue and once again was taken to the doctor. This time he took blood tests and discovered that she had diabetes. Her diet was changed and insulin prescribed, and now she is once more feeling her energetic self.

In an article entitled "Sometimes, You Have to Be Pushy," Victor Cohn cites the example given by a woman whose father had a basal cell carcinoma on the side of his nose:

> "So I asked about a dermatologist, and the home (her father's residence) called one in. When the report came back, the pathologist sent my husband a copy. My husband was a pathology professor, and he could tell from the report that the dermatologist hadn't gone far enough. There was cancer right out to the edges of the sample, posing a risk to some cells beyond it.

"I called the dermatologist, and he said, 'What are you worried about? Your father's 85.'

"I said with some restraint, 'But he would like to keep his nose. He thinks he's going to live to be 100.'"[21]

In another article entitled "Age Won't Kill You," Larry Thompson points out that it is not aging which makes us feel miserable, but disease, which needs to be understood and treated no matter what the age of the patient. His example was a ninety-five-year-old man who told his doctor that he had pain in his right knee, and that it hurt when he moved it:

> The doctor looked at him and said, "You're 95 years old. You're bound to have some pain in your right knee. That's what happens when you get old."
>
> But the man was smart. He replied, "But my left knee is 95 years old too, and it's just fine."[22]

I find it frightening for us all that the aches and pains of the old are not taken seriously. Alex Comfort, that wonderfully assuring man writing on the folklore and nonsensical attitudes toward old age, stated that the salient fact is obvious enough. "'Old' people are people who have lived a certain number of years, and *that is all*. If they have physical problems, so do younger people."[23] In these words Dr. Comfort challenges his readers to give heed:

> As an "old" person, you will need four things—dignity, money, proper medical services and useful work. They are exactly the things you always needed. As things are today, you won't get them, but there is no divinely ordered reason why you should not. So, either set out now to see that you do get them or work to force society to change its posture—or do both.[24]

Doctor Comfort does not fail to deal forcefully with the important issue of vocation, recognizing that work is as important to the old as to the young:

The real curse of being old is the ejection from a citizenship traditionally based on work. In other words it is a demeaning idleness, nonuse, not being called on any longer to contribute, and hence being put down as a spent person of no public account, instructed to run away and play until death comes out to call us to bed. . . . There is in fact marginally more chance of useful social involvement for an old person in a ghetto than for a retired executive pitched into a life of uninterrupted golf or reading paperbacks, who may not recognize that he has been sold a second, noncivic childhood along with the condominium key.[25]

And then there is the terrible plight of those in nursing homes. Most of us who have visited them do not like what we see, and are filled with dread if we think about being a patient in such a place. One of the worst things that happens to old people in nursing homes is that grief and rage are muffled, if not obliterated, by the indiscriminate use of tranquilizers. Though they are stricken in every way, residents in homes for the old are not permitted to mourn or to be angry. They have usually lost everything—home, work, family, their place in the larger community, health, movement, beauty, control, choice, privacy—a sense of their own worth. They are the Jobs of the world, but they lack Job's friends. His friends may not have been perfect comforters, but they had the grace to sit silently with him for seven days and seven nights. ". . . and none of them said a word to him; for they saw that his suffering was very great" (Job 2:13, NEB). Which of us would care so much and know so much about the need of the human heart?

As a counselor I have taken note: Job's friends waited for him to break the silence. They waited until the despairing and alienated Job was restored to trust. He opened his mouth and all his dammed up feelings poured forth in torrential grief.

> Every terror that haunted me has caught up with me,
> and all that I feared has come upon me.

There is no peace of mind nor quiet for me;
I chafe in torment and have no rest.

Job 3:24–26, NEB

If, in the long run, his friends did prove to be poor companions, to their everlasting credit they never withdrew from the dialogue. Though angered and offended by Job's raving, they did not drug his mind and block his descent into the depths of his despairing heart. Whosoever deters another from making that journey into the dark blocks out the light that is reported to shine in the darkness.

Though sixty-six I am slow to acknowledge that I am in the first stage of old age which, incidentally, has as many stages as childhood, a fact that we would discover if we gave our aging any considered attention. I am more at peace than at any other time in my life, not, however, because old age is in itself peaceful. Contrary to our stereotyping, this period is often a time of great turmoil and intensity.

I never promise those whom I counsel that the next stage of life will be easier. The fact is that each new stage is harder than the one that went before. Each asks that we let go our grasp on what is and plunge into the terrors and promises of the unknown. Once I thought that the hardest stage was saved for the very last because in old age we were expected to have the inner resources for that most incredible of all times in life. Now I am not so sure. An illness or a great blow can overnight wipe out large inner resources and leave us without power to act or resist. Our work then will be to share in the work of Christ on the cross—to keep our innermost being open to the transforming power of suffering. I do not imagine that anyone is ever ready for that work in advance of it, or that it can ever be prescribed for another.

Perhaps the work of every stage like the work of every day is learning how to live, finding the path that is one's own path, and doing whatever is necessary to follow that way.

16

The Hulled Heart

Today in an early morning dream I was addressed by a voice. It asked, "What are you doing?" and I answered, "I am hulling my heart." The voice asked "Why?" and I answered, "I have need of a hulled heart."

I awoke, as I have so often this year, knowing that in my sleep I was at work on my life, convinced that if I dug in its soil long enough, deep enough, it would yield me a liberating truth. Is that truth in the metaphor "hulled heart"? I think only of pulling off the green leaves of strawberries that the fruit may be eaten. But hulling means more than that. We strip corn and peas of husks and pods to reach the inner fruit. What are the hard, protective casings around my heart that must be stripped away to reach the hidden grain? What must I give up to lie all bare and exposed like peas in a pod or corn on a cob? What are the wrappings that keep the essence of my life from becoming bread for the world? "This is my body broken for you. Eat you all of it."

All this year old occupations have not had the same meaning. They are husks that wrap me too tight around. I want to throw them off in one grand gesture, but I am afraid of falling into the ground and dying. I am afraid of discarding the threadbare garments I huddle in for fear that I will stand cold and shivering in the dark, waiting for an angel that may not come. Nevertheless I am haunted by the biblical fact that it was the people who sat in darkness who saw a great light.

17

Enough to Go Around

Today I went through a deteriorating building near The Potter's House that had the possibility of being converted into a resident care center for older persons. The inflated price was $600,000. We have no money for this purpose. The Potter's House is engaged in raising $100,000 to make the next payment on its mortgage, and The Columbia Road Health Service is trying to raise $83,000 so that it can do the necessary renovation work in its new location. Other missions are engaged in similar fund-raising programs. Another effort for still another project might be foolish to consider. I mentioned this to Gordon Cosby, but he was not in the least concerned by such a consideration. He never feels that any one of our projects vies with any other for either money or people, though from time to time I have that nagging thought, ill-founded as it may be. The unhampered proliferation of missions in this community would not have been possible without the encouragement and care of this man. To be sure, the new always attracts life and generates an excitement that stirs envy, but that is no reason to be afraid. Our experience overwhelmingly indicates that the missions enhance one another rather than compete with one another. Many times a person, unsure what her call in life is, will go from one mission to another. She gives each the gift of her energies for a time, but then she has to try others in an effort to discover the one that connects with something deep in herself and which can become for her true vocation.

A Darwinian view of life makes us feel threatened by developing people and projects and nations. This view may have its place, but it is quite apart from a more spiritual understanding which sees each person and center of life as an integral part of the whole and without which any mission would be incomplete. If my artist friend never discovers he is an artist, then I will never have his paintings—only his discontent. But that can be the head's reasoning alone. The dread of loss in me is rooted in another place and listens to other voices.

If our dreams are to take form, money will be essential, but even more important is leadership. When I think earnestly about that I become uneasy. I am unsure of my commitment to a project for the elderly. Nonetheless, with Bob Boulter's help I arranged to be shown through the building. From past experience I know that when I begin investing myself in a dream or in a life, the commitment grows. Where I put my energies and my treasure, my reluctant heart sometimes follows. If any of us had to be fully committed when starting out, very little would ever be begun. It would be like having to decide to marry on the first meeting. What we have to do is to take one step and, if it seems good, take another.

The building is in such a state of deterioration that it would have to be completely gutted to be made habitable by anyone. I should not say this because the fact is that the roach- and rat-infested rooms gave evidence that street people are living there now. At the end of the tour Jim O'Brien, our adviser in real estate matters, told me that it was unlikely the place would accommodate forty persons. He suggested that I put my vision in writing on one page so that he could have the building appraised by architects. When I took care to say that I was not fully committed to the project he seemed unconcerned. To have this knowledgeable man take time from his work in the middle of the day to test the reality of a dream gave me a singing feeling.

Many things happen in the communities of The Church of The Saviour because there are people around who do not think large undertakings are beyond the accomplishment of ordinary people. "If it were impossible," said Gordon, "you would not be able to envision it." If he is right, that would be a very great truth to take root in one. I have tried since to envision something that would be impossible, and I have thought of nothing.

Putting in writing my dream of a residential center for older persons was a good exercise, and seems worth including here even if I am not the one to give this vision form.

1 8

Sarah's Circle— A Vision for the Elderly

Unless we are old already, the next "old people" will be us. Whether we go along with the kind of treatment meted out to those who are now old depends upon how far society can sell us the bill of goods it sold them—and it depends more upon that than upon any research. No pill or regime known, or likely, could transform the latter years of life as fully as could a change in our vision of age and a militancy in attaining that change.[26]

Alex Comfort

Sarah's Circle will be a residential community which seeks to meet the needs and call out the potential of older persons, with a special focus on the elderly poor. The community is being planned by members of The Church of The Saviour of Washington, D.C., along with inner city residents.

Sarah's Circle takes its name from the biblical Sarah who, rejoicing in the son that she bore to Abraham in his old age, exclaimed, "God has given me cause to laugh; all those who hear of it will laugh with me." She even named her son Isaac, which in Hebrew means laughter. Sarah's Circle is envisioned as a place of new birth and laughter.

The mission of Sarah's Circle will be to confront the spirit-crippling stereotypes of aging, and the tragic fact that more than four million older Americans are struggling to survive on incomes below the poverty level. Another four million of the elderly fight for some semblance of existence on incomes very close to that arbitrary "poverty line," called by some an "inadequate and miserly measure of suffering."

These figures cloak the grim reality that the people trying to eke out their lives on such low incomes spend a disproportionate amount of their money on unsuitable housing which is, nevertheless, expensive. Moreover, at a time of diminishing strength and growing disability, they have little access to adequate health care. More devastating than ill health, however, is loneliness. Denied work, and cut off from any real involvement in the world they must live in, the forgotten poor spend their long days in dismal, low-rent rooming houses or are forced onto the streets. Others, more financially independent, are warehoused in "rest" or "nursing" homes where they suffer from neglect or become the easy victims of drug abuse.

Sarah's Circle will offer hope and choice for a group traditionally denied both. More than anything, however, it will build a small community of caring, where persons of different backgrounds, races, and needs agree to struggle for a common life that is marked by creativity, birthings, and transformation. Everybody's gift will be evoked and everyone will be assisted in finding a good work to do. It will not matter if a resident has not read, or voted, or loved, or laughed before coming to Sarah's Circle. To the left of Christ on the Cross was a thief who, having gained the Kingdom at the last moment, gave to us all the message that it is never too late.

Sarah's message is the same, "Who would have told Abraham that Sarah would nurse children; yet I have borne him a child in his old age." Frederick Buechner, commenting on that astonishing couple, wrote:

Sarah and her husband had had plenty of hard knocks in their time, and there were plenty more of them still to come, but at that moment when the angel told them they'd better start dipping into their old age pensions for cash to build a nursery, the reason they laughed was that it suddenly dawned on them that the wildest dreams they'd ever had hadn't been half wild enough.[27]

Circles within the Circle

Residents in Sarah's Circle will be given the opportunity to be in a small growth circle made up of eight to twelve persons meeting under trained volunteer leaders. Participants will tell their stories as well as work with interpersonal relationships and the whole area of the emotional life. They will have the opportunity to "catch up" on the uncompleted tasks of other stages as well as to clarify the issues that confront us all at each new stage. Even though old age, like middle age, is beginning to receive more attention, only a few enlightened ones view it as a time of growth and development, and yet any careful observer of the life process, who is also a believer, knows that God did not err in his plan when he created so incredible a stage in life.

The small growth circle will give participants a place to work through grief experiences, to deal with conflict and with issues of abandonment, of letting go and letting be, as well as the crucial one of vocation. Each person, no matter how old, has an important work to do. The small groups will also provide a setting for participants to explore their unmet needs, as well as dreams and hopes for the future, and yearnings and gifts to be actualized.

Residents of Sarah's Circle will learn to be builders and enablers of one another so that each will be equipped for a healing ministry to a wounded world. The small growth groups can be a paradigm for healing in all the oppressive institutions of the land. In one sense they will be training for the priesthood—every one a minister—as is any experience which helps us to stand on the holy ground of our own lives.

In preparation for giving leadership in these small groups the core members of Sarah's Circle will themselves meet weekly with a group therapist—another step on the continuous journey of becoming fishers of men and women, moving toward a time when every person has the opportunity to be caught up in a small net of caring. If the message and the model seem somewhat unusual, think how it must have sounded in the year 30 A.D. when a strange young man with a so-called "promising future" decided to throw it all away and cast his lot for better or for worse with a circle of twelve. To anyone looking on, it could not have seemed that that little group would ever amount to much.

The Breaking of Bread
One of the Dynamics of Sarah's Circle

Matthew Fox has urged us all to change from the overly competitive and self-centered mystical symbol of "climbing Jacob's ladder" to the symbol of interdependence, creativity, humor, and gentle loving characterized by the Sarah's circle he describes:

> . . . Sarah's circle symbolizes a dynamic that has been among us for a long time though we had never named it as such. It is present, for example, wherever eating with others is of importance. After all, when we invite someone over for dinner, we do not climb a ladder and drop crumbs on them, much less pour drinks from that height. We talk of "sitting around the table"— even when the table is oblong—for sitting and eating together is a Sarah's circle experience. It is sensual and earthy, all are eye-to-eye; it is interdependent ("please pass me the jam"), and yet not dependent; it is shared fun, shared conversation and shared ecstasy (provided the cook is adequate to the occasion). Wherever there is true conviviality (Illich's phrase) as in dining together, there is Sarah's circle in action.[28]

At the center of Sarah's Circle will be a warm and gracious dining room where residents will share at least one meal a day with staff and friends. With its emphasis on wholeness, Sarah's Circle will give special attention to the importance of good nutrition in keeping folk healthy as well as in restoring health when it has been impaired. Just as poor food can make us ill, good food can heal us. The meals served in the dining room will always be natural and wholesome—another means of affirming our connection with the nurturing earth and God's love.

The dining room will be large enough to accommodate banquets and to celebrate festival days with special feasts. Celebrating is going to be something that Sarah's Circle will do with great frequency. The precedence for such carrying on is a Galilean who loved to eat with his companions whether it was in the morning or at night, on a hillside or at a wedding. He believed that people become known to one another in the breaking of bread; for this reason he wanted his memorial to be a supper, and broke bread with his disciples in the Upper Room and on the Emmaus Road. Later on he prepared a meal for them on a beach. When he said, "Come and breakfast" (John 21:12), his friends recognized him. At such an hour as that—with their betrayal of him still a fresh pain, with their fondest hopes dashed, and any thought of the future all but unbearable—who but he would have suggested that they have a fish fry. Jesus was aware that in the deep heart of each of us is a yearning for the healing intimacy that comes with the shared meal. "Look, I am standing at the door, knocking. If one of you hears me calling and opens the door, I will come in to share his meal, side by side with him" (Rev. 3:20).

An Educational Center

Sarah's Circle will be an educational center for residents and the neighborhood. The classes offered will minister to the whole person—to the spiritual, historical, intellectual, emotional, and physical facets of our multi-dimensional beings. Participants will be taught how to keep journals or tape record their thoughts, feelings, and responses. They will share their individual stories—the history of their particular households and regions of the country. An important emphasis will be the neglected area of defining and understanding the developmental stages of elderhood.

Basic to the concept of Sarah's Circle is the conviction that the generations need each other. So often growth is stunted for lack of the gifts that only different ages can give to each other. The very old person and the very young person need the touch and the sight of one another. One is the Alpha, the other the Omega that every circle requires for completeness. As a gift to itself, the neighborhood, and the city, Sarah's Circle will offer classes in child development, parenting, and grandparenting. Children, residents, staff, and neighborhood will be nurtured in the concept of life as pilgrimage, intended to be from beginning to end a walk toward liberation, toward the freedom to love and to care.

The vision of Sarah's Circle embraces the inward journey where persons come to know themselves, and the outward journey where they participate in building the earth. Instructors and guides for the two journeys will be drawn from The Church of The Saviour community, local universities and seminaries, and will include some of the residents themselves. From time to time we hope to have a scholar or researcher in residence. Sarah's Circle will not be a place where visitors entertain the old, but a place where people go for enlightenment.

Because Sarah's Circle sees itself as an educational center, the dining room will be designed to serve as a lecture hall and theater. Drama and seminars will be presented, and three or four times a year outstanding authorities will be invited to speak on child care, aging, community and world concerns. After the presentation the audience will sit around the tables breaking bread while they exchange thoughts and ideas. On these occasions the residents will be the hosts and hostesses. The expectation is that Sarah's Circle will become known as an intellectual center and the birthing place of the new.

Let the unbelieving consider the words that Sarah spoke:

> Who would have told Abraham
> that Sarah would nurse children!
> Yet I have borne him a child in his old age.
> Genesis 21:7

19

Two Worlds

Today Kwasi came to see me. Two weeks ago he returned from a visit to his home country of Ghana, and he wanted someone with whom to share his agony about the sufferings of his people.

He said, "You can cross the land of Ghana and not find soap. Our currency is cedis, but it is worthless in other countries, so there is a black market on dollars. The exchange rate is four cedis for one dollar, but on the black market they give sixty cedis, because across the boarder with one dollar you can buy four cakes of soap." The wonder of soap. I have always taken it for granted. Water and soap, a clean body, clean hair, clean clothes. Only once before have I marveled over the miracle gift of soap and water and that was when I was in a refugee camp on the Thai border. Soap was given out sparingly with one bucket of water a day to each person. With that bucket the family did its cooking, its laundry, and its bathing.

"When I was home last time," Kwasi said, "I took many things with me. This time my aunt had died and I did not have time to make adequate preparation for a trip. I was visiting my country with very little money, and because I did not have enough I could see the depth of the misery of my people. I had to live the old life. I had forgotten how bad it was, and now it had become worse.

"When I went to my own family, I had been away so long I was a special guest. They had half of a fish and they served it to me. The children two to seven years old were not allowed to come close to the table because this was special food for a special person. It would make you very sad. A little portion of food the size of a tennis ball, and six children scratching each other to get at it.

"When I went to a neighboring country (Nigeria) and came back my mother wept the whole day because I had a can of corned beef. She feels I would not have a can of beef, if I had not been looting. At home a little can of sardines is a luxury. A whole family of eight will eat it. When you eat sardines in America no one thinks that you are a rich man.

"The people in my country look to America for help. I say, 'Yes, we have food in America. Everyone can have a chicken and a place to live, if they work hard, but you are afraid to go into the street. Even your neighbor might kill you.' 'What does that matter,' they say. 'If you have food to eat and a little wine to sip, you can stay in your room. Why do you have to go out?' All the time I was in Ghana there was not a single robbery or any crime.

"The taxis there are ten to twelve years old. The doors have no glass, and they do not close. When the taxis break down there are no parts. If you need brake fluid or engine oil you have to wait until someone brings it to you from another country.

"Transportation is a large problem. You stand in the scorching sun for three or four hours and there is no sign of transportation. Imagine how that must be for a man and woman with children. One day I waited half the day for a taxi. When the taxi came and I got on, too many people got on with me. That is always the way. One foot was in and one foot hanging out. My shoe falls from the foot hanging out. Never mind that, but the foot is still outside. When I call, the driver stops and lets me off to get the shoe, but when I return with the shoe someone has my place.

"The papers for my return were difficult to process, so I had to stay for many months. I had to live the old life. It was very hard, and now when I think of my family there is a great pain in me."

Kwasi is paid four dollars an hour for hotel work. On this he supports himself, goes to school, and saves money to send back home. Like the Vietnamese, Salvadorans, and many others in this city he cannot forget the abject misery of his kinfolk.

Like Kwasi, I, too, live in two worlds. Only yesterday I returned once more from visiting with Richard. Until I make the trip again, I will with each passing day gain emotional distance from him. The pain will recede and his suffering life will not intrude upon my thoughts so often. But today he is scarcely out of mind. Long ago schizophrenia, that most dreaded of all mental illnesses, shattered his thoughts and robbed him of words to say what is happening to him. All I know is that in this life he is out of the reach of human warmth and comfort, condemned to listening to voices that no one else hears—to a world of distortion and sometimes terror that must be what hell is like. And yet, one still sees in countless flashes the whole person, as though that person were some place, all intact.

I have struggled to overcome my identification with this brother of mine as though the sadness in me were a betrayal of the joy of Christ. The warfare has been of a losing kind—a battle I will never win, especially at the Christmas season. A part of me is engaged in festive parties and holiday dinners and prayers of praise to God the Mother, God the Father, who came to us in Jesus Christ, while another part of me lives in the bare halls of mental institutions and on the streets of a thousand cities—alone, ill-clothed, ill-fed, confused, and afraid. I know now that the peace of Christmas is found in bringing these two worlds together. He came to bring "peace to you who were far off and peace to those who were near . . ." (Eph. 2:17, RSV).

The One whose birthday we celebrate is the One who was so identified with the broken and the hurt that he could say ". . . I was naked and you clothed me, sick and you visited me, in prison and you came to see me" (Matt. 25:36–37). Surely this is an extreme kind of identification with the afflicted. Though some would label it pathological, what he was trying to teach was an at-oneness with himself and with the poor, ". . . in so far as you neglected to do this to one of the least of these, you neglected to do it to me" (Matt. 25:45). He wanted us to know that he was bread and wine—that His life could flow into us. "For to me to live is Christ" (Phil. 1:21, RSV).

A friend once said to me, "I do not help someone in a pit by climbing down into the pit with him." It sounded wise at the time. But on reflection I know that no one ever knows what it is like in the pit except by climbing down into it. "When it says, 'he ascended,' what can it mean if not that he descended right down to the lower regions of the earth?" (Eph. 4:9). The real feat is not to lose one's separateness so that one can ascend again and throw to the other whatever kind of rope is needed. That is the important achievement.

The life of Moses was forever altered because one day he wandered down from the palace to watch his kinfolk at their hard labor. Even in a new land whenever he returned to the deeps of himself he found waiting there for him another kind of world full of long-suffering. He had the task of healing the split within himself—of bringing his two worlds together. I have that same task as have Kwasi and all the refugees who jam our cities and countrysides. I suspect that many who carry pain in their hearts have that same work of bringing two worlds together.

We stand at a pivotal point in world history. If we will but listen to the cries of the alienated and despairing among us, we may be able to journey down from protected places of pride and prejudice, look at the divisions within ourselves, and find the oppressive structures that afflict us whether they are in the inner fabric of our lives, in our family household, or in the larger society. This is where we can join God's liberation movement. This is where we can yoke ourselves with the Stranger who lives within us.

20

On Hearing Call

Thinking about the homeless of the world and about Kwasi and the call he feels upon his life, I find myself pondering the whole subject of call. It is such a rich topic that my thoughts fall over one another. So much I would like to say and yet so much eludes me. I feel as though I am contemplating mystery. Time was when I thought that the all-important subject was gifts, and that, if only we could identify our gifts, and begin using them, our lives would burst with creativity and the world would be restored. Now I am not so sure. A talent may be so great that it propels a person forever down one path, as is the case with some artists. But even for these extraordinary folk, call determines whether and how they use their gifts. A writer can produce advertising copy, history, propaganda, poetry, contracts and proposals, political speeches, or sermons.

If one day I should be called to bring into being a residential center for some of the city's homeless—and some days I think this is my call—then I might never write again, not because writing had ceased to be an important gift or to make claims upon me, but because other gifts more needed in the fulfillment of the new call would be evoked and take precedence. To be deeply nurturing and to carry one's life into the future, the use of a gift must be related to what one is called to do. An authentic call is hard to discern in today's world, a fact that makes difficult the naming and using of our gifts. Gifts evolve in response to call, and we may not yet have heard a call.

Difficulty in hearing and understanding the nature of call arises from the fact that we give it so little attention. I grew up in the cold and hungry depression years before World War II when the main goal in life was to find a job. It did not matter much what the job was. The essential thing was to have work that one went to in the morning and returned from at night. This is still true for vast numbers today. Where a choice is possible it is not exercised. The individual is not inner directed but influenced by salary, prestige, future opportunities, the chance leading of friends, not to mention the conscious and unconscious wishes of parents, so that even people who appear to be privileged are rarely doing work that is related to call.

Finding a job is quite different from finding one's vocation, a word having its origin in the Latin infinitive *vocare*, to call, from which comes *vocatio*, meaning a bidding or invitation. It implies a summoning voice which comes from above one, and at the same time sounds deep within one's being. The uninitiated need more help in discerning that voice than most modern guides offer. Can it be said today as it was said in the days of Samuel, God rarely speaks and visions are uncommon (1 Sam. 3:1)? Samuel was fortunate in that there was someone available to give him proper instructions. To begin with he was "lying in the sanctuary of Yahweh where the ark of God was, when Yahweh called, 'Samuel! Samuel!' He answered, 'Here I am.' Then he ran to Eli and said, 'Here I am, since you called me.' Eli said, 'I did not call. Go back and lie down.' So he went and lay down. Once again Yahweh called, 'Samuel! Samuel!' Samuel got up and went to Eli and said, 'Here I am, since you called me.' Eli then understood that it was Yahweh who was calling the boy, and he said to Samuel, 'Go and lie down, and if someone calls say, 'Speak, Yahweh, your servant is listening.' So Samuel went and lay down in his place" (1 Sam. 3:3-9).

When the Lord called again, Samuel answered, "Speak, Yahweh, your servant is listening." Yahweh spoke then and Samuel caught a vision of the future.

To hear and discern the voice of God, one has to be in a state of attention with one's ear turned inward. The difficulty is that we are not often in a receptive posture. The only time I ever lay down in a sanctuary was that night at the Luther Place Memorial Church where the street women slept in dorm-like rooms behind the sanctuary. Once during the night the volunteers go into the dark sanctuary for an hour and stretch out beneath the tall stained glass windows. If I were to spend enough time lying in the immense quiet of that room I believe that I, too, might hear a voice calling. I might even one day respond, "Speak, Yahweh, your servant is listening."

Although call is a dominant note in Scriptures, we rarely give it serious consideration, so that for many the whole subject has an esoteric sound. As a result, call is seldom discussed in this society. We sometimes ask small children what they want to be when they grow up, but we rarely take their answers seriously, or help them to elaborate on and to enter into their images—essential preparation for the nurturing of imagination and the hearing of call. By using one's imaginative power one is able to behold what is not seen by ordinary sight, and to hear words which usually fall to the ground. This is why William Blake equated imagination with salvation. "This world of imagination is the world of Eternity."[29]

If imagination were to be exercised and visions were to become more common, we would hear much talk about call. As it is now, even in the church, it is not normal for people to speak about it. As a rule the church recognizes one call—the call to the professional ministry. Whereas, if the church were true to herself, she would help all her people to discern and be faithful to call. In such an effort, however, institutions probably recognize a threat to their own structures. When individuals become autonomous persons, in touch with resources of latent energy deep within themselves, they can no longer be contained within neat boundaries. If church people begin listening to call, those we count on most will likely be off on some wild adventures of their own. Some of the tasks that we have depended on lay persons to do may not get done. Similar fears come up in marriages. One friend said, "The more I had my own projects, the less time I had for my husband's projects. I began to fear that he would find someone else."

Call more often than not is bound up with economic risks, and often does not seem very prudent to those looking on. A journey is also involved. Call asks that we set out from a place that is familiar and relatively secure for a destination that can be only dimly perceived, and that we cannot be at all certain of reaching, so many are the obstacles that will loom along the way. One of the ways to test the authenticity of call is to determine whether it requires a journey. This journey is not necessarily geographical although, as in the case of Abraham and Moses, it is not at all unusual for it to involve leaving one's work and home. Whether or not the call includes an outward journey, it always requires an inward one. We need to be delivered from all that binds and keeps the real self from breaking into music and becoming joy to the world.

The first stretch of the inward journey is touching in some vital way our own deepest feelings. To see visions or to hear call without being faithful to one's most ardent yearnings is utterly impossible. Our strongest feelings revolve around our wants and desires, and we have been taught since our first summer to give these only slight attention, so that when we think about drawing close to our real longings we have feelings of guilt and shame. It is as though our deepest wishes were unworthy and, if pursued, would get us into all kinds of trouble, and at the very least cause us to feel or be called selfish. The opposite, of course, is true.

When we succeed in ignoring our wants they either find expression in destructive ways or cause us all kinds of ills and problems that make us self-centered and self-serving—the very end we are so anxious to avoid. The outcome, however, is not usually this dramatic. Out of touch with the life-giving energy of our wants and desires, we are more apt to become flat and uninteresting people. Imperceptibly disintegration goes on at the very core of life. The calm and expressionless face reflects not peace at the center, but a dying going on within.

For these passionless selves the words were spoken, "Awake, O sleeper, and arise from the dead, and Christ will give you light" (Eph. 5:14, RSV).

Could the way back to that "long long ago, when wishing still could lead to something,"[30] be to move into the pain that each of us carries inside? So much of life is spent in trying to keep up, or keep going rather than in experiencing and reflecting on what is happening within and around us. As soon as we become ill we reach for, and are given medicine that will keep us functioning. Only a rare doctor ever asks a patient to reflect on what might be causing the illness. In like manner we handle our psychic aches—avoiding any honest encounter with them by finding other occupations to fill our day. This may be good economy of resources in the matter of small griefs and problems. Time seems to heal them as the proverb says.

The larger sorrows do not so readily go away, and may be intricately related to the work we are to do. I find this teaching in the biographies I read. Alexander Bell, so concerned that the human voice be heard around the world, had a deaf mother and a deaf wife. Thomas Edison, when asked if he had any fears, replied "I fear the dark."

Sigmund Freud, who uncovered the Oedipus complex, had a constricting relationship with a dominating mother, while Carl Jung, who introduced a fresh spirituality into psychoanalysis as well as into religion, struggled against being smothered by the church's rules and theological teachings represented in his own household by his father, a rigid Presbyterian minister. Many of the counselors I know grew up in troubled households and turned to therapy to resolve their own conflict.

David, a twelve-year-old boy who lived all but the last two weeks of his life in a germ-free bubble because he was born without immunity to disease, had a keen interest in medicine and space. Thomas Jarman, considered by many to have been the world's greatest legal expert on wills, died without one. We sometimes teach the things we need to learn. Or is it that we heal others in the way we either need to be healed, or have been healed?

Henry Kaplan, whose pioneering research in radiation treatment prolonged life for thousands of cancer victims, and changed Hodgkin's disease from hopeless to curable, died of lung cancer. At the age of fifteen, when his father died of lung cancer, he set forth on his path as a cancer specialist.

Although my research is limited and not at all scientific, for me it is conclusive evidence that, at the center of our pain, we glimpse a fairer world and hear a call. When we are able to keep company with our own fears and sorrows, we are shown the way to go; our own parched lives are watered and the earth becomes a greener place.

The relationship between pain and vocation first became clear to me when I was reading books on child development. In one book an author stated matter-of-factly that play is to a child what work is to an adult. In a very different book on play therapy another author explained how, in arranging dolls and toy furniture, the child expresses her inner conflicts and her struggle to work them out. Is it possible that the adult, when working at what he wants to do, is also engaged in the same process? For such an adult his work becomes his play. Through that work not only is he healed, but he becomes a healer. It might be said that in finding vocation one discovers how to be at play in the world.

At first it seems odd that the things that grieve us may hold God's address to us. On deeper consideration, however, it almost has to be that way. On the ground of our most grievous ache, where we feel powerless to free or heal ourselves, we cry out, "What must I do to be saved?" That is the place of meeting with Christ who is Lord and Savior. There we are given a new vision to reach toward.

Then I saw *a new heaven and a new earth;* the first heaven and the first earth had disappeared now, and there was no longer any sea. I saw the holy city, and the new Jerusalem, coming down from God out of heaven, as beautiful as a bride all dressed for her husband. Then I heard a loud voice call from the throne, "You see this city? Here God lives among men. He will make *his home among them; they shall be his people,* and he will be their God; his name is *God-with-them. He will wipe away all tears from their eyes;* there will be no more death, and no more mourning or sadness. The world of the past has gone" (Rev. 21:1–4).

Hope begins to grow and we are summoned to the work that will give us a feeling of wellness, and make possible that which we envision.

If it is true that each of us has a work to do which will make us feel well when we are doing it, then there is nothing more important than finding that work. Attention to call becomes urgent. Moreover, preventing another from following what he is sighing after becomes a grievous sin. Frustration, impotence, and rage fill the heart that cannot be about its real business, which is always the Father's business. Call, like imagination, is the same as salvation.

21

Resistance and Surrender to Call

Sigmund Freud, in one of his writings, said:

Every great man must overcome three kinds of difficulties: first, the resistance in himself; second, the friction and fight with his contemporaries; and third, the difficulties arising from the work itself.

Freud might have said every creator, great or small, meets with those difficulties. This is always my experience with writing. Though my mind may be cluttered with the things in me that cry out to be heard, when I think about committing them to paper the resistance at the outset is terrible to encounter. I have never been able to fathom what underlies that resistance, though I can identify parts of it. Foremost is a feeling of inadequacy before the imagined work. Who am I to think that I can bring something out of nothing? God did that when the world was made and when each of us came into being, but, after all, creation is God's work. One would have to believe that she was made in the image of the great Artificer to be so bold as to think that she was a creator. To give lip service to such a belief is always easier than to act upon it. What difference does it make if once upon a time one produced a book, or a painting, or a house, and saw that it was good? That is no guarantee that one can breathe life again into words or mortar or whatever one chooses. Creation, which is never repetition, always confronts anew the formless void in one's self.

Side by side with feelings of inadequacy I find in me a strong reluctance to withdraw myself from the social life going on around me. Every creative work requires that lonely act of withdrawal which triggers a full-scale battle within myself. I don't want to cut off all those little conversations that fill my week and give me a place in the society of my friends, my church, my neighborhood, and my world. I remember reading that the poet Rainer Rilke would not take the time to go to his daughter's wedding, and finally gave his dog away because he was too much of a distraction. Though most of us struggle with the claims of a much lesser talent than his, our efforts at creation still require drawing upon powers deep within the self where the attention can then be caught in inextricable bonds. What I fiercely resist in the beginning carries me off as its quarry once the surrender is made. Afterwards, wherever I go I take with me another world that is more real than the world in which I try to live. Though I have put the work aside, a part of me remains behind as a nurturing, hovering presence.

Then there is anger. More than any other emotion anger blocks creativity. To create is to give one's self. Creativeness, always generous, is a way of loving. The world, far from recognizing this, seldom honors or rewards its artists by encouragement or makes their work easier. Rather, artistic pursuits are often viewed as egocentric, fine if they succeed, but how often does that happen? Better leave art for weekends, and use one's energies for grinding out something utilitarian that can be used to promote whatever the current fad or cause happens to be. In such a climate the creator in us is afraid to take or ask for himself time for the godly work of brooding. The risk is too great. Even though the request is granted, the chances are that one will lose one's place, become poor and isolated—angrier still. That anger becomes fuel for one's battle with one's contemporaries. When I am angry I want to withhold myself. I resist the giving of my gifts. I have to struggle to drag into the open that part of me that is holding out and lecture it on how creating, like loving, is hard only when we expect something in return. Creating, I tell my lonely, complaining self, has to be its own reward. Like loving it is a way of pouring one's life into the world, of experiencing the divinity in ourselves. Loving and creating hold a cross to be stretched upon because they are the way we become eternal.

I lift up the experience of the artist only because he presents a blown-up picture of the creator in each of us. We all long to create. We all know what it is to have the self denied by someone else, to be left lonely and helpless with one's anger, struggling with the temptation to hug one's self to one's self. Some days on Columbia Road I feel in the atmosphere the impotent rage of the young and the immense sorrow of the old who are denied the opportunity of loving and creating the earth. When we have touched that pain in ourselves we can touch it in others whether we find it in well-appointed living rooms or on ghetto streets.

But greater than these resistances is one I cannot name, and which I succeed in conquering only by a sheer, desperate act of the will. Gordon Cosby on occasion has reinforced the part of me that wanted to write by charging me ten dollars for each day that I did not give two hours to writing. I never had to produce in those two hours, but I had to stay at the typewriter and try. That penance worked in the days when I was young and poor, and would agree to it. The years have gone by since then, and it is no longer possible for either Gordon or for me to be serious about that penance, so, of course, it would not work. For lack of another in its place I am left unaided to struggle with the mysterious opposing forces in myself. The strength of them is so great that I have come to wonder whether every creative work does not have to wrest its very being from the unconscious, which is always wide and deep and reluctant to give over any of its knowledge. Darkness is always over the deep and requires a hovering spirit for there to be light. Some call that spirit the Muse. I find myself turning inward to hear a still, small voice.

In thinking about becoming a group therapist I was up against a resisting force that I had not encountered as a writer. One of my many selves still felt like a child in the world. That small and powerless self thought it ludicrous that it should be asked to assume the responsibility of leading groups when it was not capable of taking care of itself. It did not even want to try. Knowing no small fright at the thought of becoming a healer and a teacher, it wanted to go on being the child, or at least a patient or a student. Despite the suffering involved in the dependent position, that stance served a secret fantasy that had its own rewards. This Peter Pan self caused no end of conflict in me, but in the end it lost out to other stronger selves with eyes on other goals. Reluctantly, it grew up and became integrated into my inner household of grownups. A sure and quiet strength began to flow in me. For the first time in my life I felt fully adult. I understood better what it meant to be a free person as well as how easy it is to forsake the painful road to freedom. That experience also helped me to understand how response to call helps to complete something in oneself.

I find other resistances rising up in me when I think of Sarah's Circle. If I say yes to it, I say no to more idyllic dreams. I had planned to create gourmet meals in my own old age, and entertain my friends before the fireplace—pursuits my commitments have never allowed. These activities are also call. I see them as filling gaps in myself—of making me more human, more available to others. In the long winter evenings my friends and I might talk about revolutions and revolutionaries, but that is quite different from being in a revolution and being a revolutionary, and that is really what Sarah's Circle is about. It is about leading a small segment of the elderly out of their abysmal poverty into clean, safe space where food, and health care, and shelter, and work, and self-esteem are everybody's right. Sarah's Circle is about restoring the years that the locusts have eaten and empowering the old for the continuing work of creation. It is about calling America's attention to the poverty of the elderly in her midst. It is about helping each of us to face our own fears of aging, which keep us from receiving the gifts and wisdom of an older population, and cherishing ourselves as aging persons. Perhaps most of all, Sarah's Circle is about changing all the ageist stereotypes that fill us with foreboding once we become thirty and sap our sweet strength with each succeeding decade. It is about overturning the greeting card racks in all the cities and hamlets of the nation and making confetti of those millions and millions of cards that give us on our birthdays the disguised message that aging is not good. Sarah's Circle will call to account a culture based on "the obsolescence not only of things, but also of people." All of which is fine language to fire the brain, but in reality means the sweat of labor that robs the winter afternoons of idle talk and the nights of the careless sleep of the uninvolved. Freud is right—my first resistance to call is in myself. I am stuck in the materialism of our age and part of me cannot believe that my own interests are served in so large an undertaking as Sarah's

Circle. To make this commitment means letting go of all the good things to which I feel I have a right in order to begin the arduous work of communicating what is now only a vision. It means asking others to believe in what belongs to another region in order that it can become part of the common landscape.

Once one has achieved unity in one's own internal household and can move with the purity of heart that every vision demands, one is up against the second difficulty that Freud cites: the friction and fight with one's contemporaries. In his extraordinary book, *The Hero with a Thousand Faces*, Joseph Campbell presents the hard task:

> . . . How to communicate to people who insist on the exclusive evidence of their senses the message of the all-generating void? . . . Why re-enter such a world? Why attempt to make plausible, or even interesting, to men and women consumed with passion, the experience of transcendental bliss? As dreams that were momentous by night may seem simply silly in the light of day, so the poet and the prophet can discover themselves playing the idiot before a jury of sober eyes. The easy thing is to commit the whole community to the devil and retire again into the heavenly rock-dwelling, close the door, and make it fast. But if some spiritual obstetrician has meanwhile drawn the *shimenawa* across the retreat, then the work of representing eternity in time, and perceiving in time eternity, cannot be avoided.[31]

The struggle with one's contemporaries, while hard to endure, is easy to understand. When we are dissatisfied with things as they are, or suffer and know pain, we begin to imagine what the world would be like if things were different—if there were no hunger or thirst and all tears were wiped away (Rev. 7:14). Creative imagination reaches toward God, and glimpses a new heaven and a new earth. The new reality has nothing to do with the present order. In fact, the one who responds to call seeks to put something more beautiful in the place of what she sees. This is where the friction and fight begin. Martin Luther

King was not killed because he had a dream. Dreamers are easily dismissed. He was killed because he sought to introduce into the political arena what he saw with his heart and mind. The same was true of Ghandi and of our Lord. As Jesus made clear his solidarity with the poor and his vocation to engage them in a liberating process, he came into confrontation with entrenched political and religious powers. As suspicion of him turned to resistance and then to hatred and fury, he began to prepare his disciples for what he would have to suffer. Peter immediately took Jesus aside to protest his continuing on what was surely a collision course. His plea might have even caused Jesus to waiver momentarily in his intent. Why else the painful cry: "Get behind me, Satan! You are an obstacle in my path, because the way you think is not God's way but man's" (Matt. 16:23). Perhaps in that brief scene we have a glimpse of Jesus battling resistance not only in society and in his small intimate circle, but in himself.

Those who say yes to the perilous vocation of implementing vision at each stage will find new resistances emerging in themselves as well as in the society. Opposition to the new is very natural and should not cause any of us to be taken by surprise. The best way to understand it in one's contemporaries is to have named and owned it in one's self. That process is also some protection against the self-righteousness that plagues too many reformers as well as the pious. The work of creativity is to unify the opposites in one's self. We know with our heads that this is our true vocation, but we need the poets to understand it with our hearts. William Blake helps me with a single line addressed to a Tyger—"Did he who made the Lamb make thee?"[32]

The war between the opposites and reconciliation between them are the great themes of Scripture often presented under the heading of temptation. The Jesus who walks through the gospels is not above the struggle to wed the contraries in himself. The Scriptures make that clear again and again. They emphasize the humanness of Jesus so that we can trust him to know our human struggle. "For it was not the angels that he took to himself; he took to himself *descent from Abraham*. It was essential that he should in this way become completely like his brothers so that he could be a compassionate and trustworthy high priest of God's religion, able to atone for human sins" (Heb. 2:16). When the humanness of Jesus is missing from God's religion we cannot understand the revolutionary implication of those statements that the mystics make concerning our vocation to be Christ.

> In a flash, at a trumpet crash,
> I am all at once what Christ is,
> Since he was what I am.[33]

Freud said that the third difficulty of the great man is found in the work itself. He does not elaborate on this statement any more than he elaborated on the first two. My guess is that he had in mind the sheer labor of a Michelangelo who for four years spent his working days lying on his back on scaffolding suspended beneath a dome no one had ever heard of; or perhaps he was thinking of the sculptor who labors to free the forms hidden in stone, or the writer trying to make words correspond with an inner reality, or the legislator engaging in the hundreds of little conversations that might make possible the passing of a new law.

The creator must be sustained by the vision that first quickened his spirit. In all the secret stages of a work's development one must believe in the promise:

> . . . the child in my womb leaped for joy. Yes, blessed is she who believed that the promise made her by the Lord would be fulfilled.
>
> Luke 1:44–45

22

Helpers and Guides along the Way

Everything I write about call has been borne out in my own life, in the books that are stacked up around me and in all those that I reach for on the shelves of libraries. I have struggled with three calls in my life: the call to be a writer, the call to be a therapist, and the call to build an institution of caring for a segment of the world which has "no place."

My call to writing came to me as a teenager. I read John Steinbeck's story of migrant workers in *Grapes of Wrath*,[34] and lived the agony of the sharecroppers in their search for food and work. In a scene toward the end of the book a nursing mother offered her breast to a starving old man. I wanted a world with that kind of caring in it. The author had opened my heart to a greater love, and I thought I might be able to use words to do the same thing for others. I fervently believed then as I do now that if we each knew how the other felt inside we would know how to be parents to one another, or priests.

Today a letter from a friend gave me another view of the world I caught a vision of that day so long ago. She wrote:

> I had a beautiful sign from nature this morning. I was writing and I looked out my window, saw a wonderful group of cedar wax-wings gathered in a tree. I rarely see them. They pass through at this time of year to gather the red berries off the evergreen bushes. Why was I seeing them? I then remembered what an ornithologist told me about cedar wax-wings: They will line up in a row, and the first bird will take a red berry and pass it along to the end of the row where the last bird is allowed to eat the berry.

Joseph Campbell writes that those who do not refuse the call are given supernatural aid:

In fairy lore it may be some little fellow of the wood, some wizard, hermit, shepherd, or smith, who appears to supply the amulets and advice that the hero will require. The higher mythologies develop the role in the great figure of the guide, the teacher, the ferryman, the conductor of souls to the afterworld. In classical myth this is Hermes-Mercury; in Egyptian, usually Thoth (the ibis god, the baboon god); in Christian, the Holy Ghost . . .[35]

"One has only to know and trust," writes Campbell, "and the ageless guardians will appear." I want to answer back, "I believe, I believe!" and to shout to all the cringing populations of the fearful earth, "It will happen for you, too." This has always been my experience. When I have felt most alone and despairing, the guide I needed for my own heroine's journey appeared. In high school it was a teacher who put into my hands the great works of literature. She took very little note of me, but she passed on her own love of her subject, which is the most important gift a teacher can give to a student.

I was eighteen before my next real helper appeared. He was an out-of-work writer who was employed by the WPA (Work Projects Administration) to teach a class in short story writing. His classroom was in a public high school along the Third Avenue El on the lower East Side of New York City. Members of the class covered a wide range of ages. Most of them were employed in offices; a few were laborers, and some had no jobs. We all shared and were bound together by the dream that we might learn the art of writing publishable stories. Each session began with a time of instruction in the writer's craft.

The first night I knew that the teacher was a strong and gifted personality with energy from invisible regions, though in those days I would not have explained it that way. From the beginning it was also clear that he took his subject seriously, would tolerate no dabblers, and would be a stern taskmaster of the disciplines he taught. We talked about these matters in the hallways as though we were once again school-children. Each night in a harsh and resonant voice he would call on someone to read his or her manuscript. Always in the course of the reading the El train would roar down the tracks, drowning the reader's voice. The god-teacher would shout the stern command, "Louder! Louder!" The quivering student would raise his voice, but never enough; the teacher would shout again, "Louder! Louder!" The reader was usually screaming as the trains rushed by.

I knew my voice would never be heard above the trains, and my extreme timidity magnified the size of this particular dragon in my path. I both longed to read my story for this man and dreaded the calling of my name. When my turn came it was a steamy August night, the hottest of the year. I was on page two when the train began descending on us. As it drew nearer, Albert—that was this god's name—instead of shouting at me, called out to the unlucky students sitting along the windows to close them, his tone suggesting that they should have had that much good sense. One by one the windows were lowered, shutting out everything until it seemed to me that only the teacher and I were left in the hot and airless room. I went home from there knowing that in that stern and eccentric man I had been sent a guide and protector.

Strangely enough the story I had read was a fantasy about vocation. Its central character was a gray little man who hated his job and took his savings to open a swap-a-job agency. It was a huge success and many branches opened. Everyone was swapping jobs. Before long the whole city was in chaos. The governor declared an emergency and ordered everyone back to his old job, but for one brief week the people of the city had whistled as they worked. There lived in me then as there does now the conviction that every human being has the right to a work that is meaningful, and that this work is different at different stages in our lives.

A few years later the war came and put an end to hunger, and to the WPA classes and the long "conversations at midnight" that would-be writers held in cluttered little restaurants beneath the El train. When the war and the long work of war were over, I moved to Washington, D.C., to help salvage my twin brother's severely damaged life. I took a job in a public relations office writing for wages. The work there made it difficult for me to be serious about my own writing, though I never stopped thinking about it. I left that job to work at The Church of The Saviour, where the promise was that I would have time to write. This was true only in small part since my job included answering a telephone that rang all the time. The most I managed to write were several pamphlets. They were enough for my next guide. When Robert Raines, who had just written *New Life in the Church,* came to visit he found the leaflets lying on a table and read them. He went home and wrote to Harper & Row telling them that The Church of The Saviour had a story to tell and someone who could tell it. After submitting an outline of ten chapters I was sent a contract to produce in nine months a book with the working title *Call to Commitment.* Publishers do not make this kind of response to unknown writers. The new evocator of my gift must have been very persuasive.

A whole week went by before I signed the contract. With the promissory piece of paper in my hands I was no longer so sure that I could write a book. Side by side with growing self-doubt was the insistent feeling that I had something to say that was intended for the whole world. The moment of surrender to the work stirring in me came in the reading of the story of Mary's pregnancy. I let her yes become my yes. If anyone asked me to define an artist or a prophet, I think that I would say that he is the one who dares to act on the bold belief that he has a word to speak that would be healing if it could be heard. Actually, all human beings way down deep hold this belief about themselves. The sorrow is that except for rare moments most of us are overcome by forces of disbelief. In time we cease to remember that our lives are for the greening of the earth and the greening of one another. We lose sight of the work we are to do, but the truth of it is hidden away in us, and makes call supremely important, lifting up as it does the healing dimension of true vocation.

In the two months after signing my first contract I made a hundred starts on the promised book, but not one of them was fit to be the opening lines. I had fallen into the pit of ambition and perfectionism. No words of mine would ever measure up to the literature that had nurtured my own life. I could not be content with me. I had yet to learn that we are not justified by the perfect work.

In October of that year I went to lead a retreat at Aldersgate Methodist Church in Ohio where Robert Raines was the minister. He greeted me with, "How is the book coming?" When I told him that I had not been able to get started he insisted that we take time to talk at the end of the retreat. I do not remember all that he said, but he gave me a piece of advice that has stood me in good stead ever since, and that I often pass on to hesitant writers: "Write it down. Don't care how it sounds. There will be plenty of time to go back and rewrite and rewrite." Partly out of desperation I was able to act on his counsel, and the words began to flow.

The greatest deterrents to the potential of creativity in this world are the standards we impose on ourselves and on others, coupled with the failure to believe in our own uniqueness and our own powers. No one is able to judge her own work—to know its value or its lack of value. Michelangelo wrote in his journal, "I am a poor man of little value, who keeps striving in that art which God has given me, to lengthen my life as much as I can." After his years of exhausting work on the Sistine vault he commented simply in a letter to his father: "I've finished that chapel I was painting. The Pope is quite satisfied."[36]

What stirs in our hearts will never correspond with what we are able to transpose onto paper or canvas or to shape into bridges and buildings and highways and institutions. Trying is all that matters. Our yes to call is saying that we will try. The guide, helper, angel, mentor, or, if you prefer, "the little fellow of the wood—some wizard, hermit, shepherd, or smith"—will appear, to supply the amulets and advice.

When the book is written, or the institution built, it will fall short, no matter how much blood it costs. Then there is nothing to do but write another book, paint another picture, start another project, dream another dream, see another vision. If it has to do with the lifting up of valleys and the leveling of mountains, the supernatural aid will be given again.

Several years ago my outrage over the treatment of the mentally ill in our society had grown so great that I thought I could no longer bear to be silent. I began trying to put my protest into words. That same week on an Amtrak train to New York I met a diligent mental health worker. Before our trip was over she offered me the copious notes she had made on conditions existing in the state institutions where her only son had committed suicide. A week later a visitor from Canada, whose severely ill husband was being released after twenty years in mental institutions, went home and copied for me reams of newspaper stories chronicling the pain and misery of mental patients and families who were unable to cope with the sudden shift in government policy. Another day, browsing at a street book stall I found a volume on the history of mental illness that could save me hours of research. I moved for a few months into a whole new realm with my ears and eyes alive to sounds and sights that were outside the usual range of my hearing and visibility. My words evoked from others responses they would not have ordinarily made.

Then something happened. My attention was captured by other concerns. For a time at least I put aside the writing of that book. The signs no longer came. No mysterious strangers appeared on my path. The days ceased to be marked by uncommon events. What was true on the outside was also true on the inside. There were no forest stretches, no mountains to scale, no boulders to push against. The landscape became flat and commonplace and nothing inward enticed me with siren strains.

When I finally became serious about my call to become a group therapist another appearance of the "mysterious helper" occurred. In one sense I had prepared all my life for this vocation, for this call had been working at subterranean levels of my being long before I was conscious of it. If this be true of all calls, then looking back we see that nothing we ever did is lost. All is preparation for the new Work. As a school girl I had devoured psychological writings, and as a very young woman in New York City I had taken all the courses in psychology that the universities offered in their evening programs. Some of these were with Karen Horney at The New School for Social Research during the period when she was founding the Association for the Advancement of Psychoanalysis. At that same time Erich Fromm, a layman, was struggling for standing room in a field that had been captured by medical doctors. I moved those years on the fringes of New York's psychologically oriented community, hanging on the words of its seers.

Even better preparation than the above, however, was the household into which I was born, and the conflicts and lostness I struggled with in my own life. Finally I found someone who listened to me over long months. In the process I became a listener. Now I know that there is no more important service in all the world than listening. We cannot be healed until we are listened to, and we cannot be healers until we know how to listen.

When the call to be a group therapist finally made itself heard in my life, I did not have one college credit to my name. No pastoral counseling institution would enroll me in its more serious programs. For a while I contented myself teaching classes emphasizing the emotional dimension of life, which seemed to me the special domain of the church. The more I listened the more convinced I became that everyone in some way is in trouble with his or her feelings. Classes would end just as participants were beginning to trust their secrets to one another and become the true confessing church. I shared my unrest with a friend, Lou Ormont, author of *The Talking Cure*, and one of New York's leading group psychoanalysts. "I will give you the additional training you need," he said. "This will require your being in New York one day a week to participate in one of my groups, and completing a program of study that I will outline.

Think in terms of at least three years." The expenditure of time and money loomed too large. I turned sadly away. My "mysterious helper" had appeared but I did not have the psychological readiness to recognize him. I still had an inward work to do.

I went on teaching and designing classes that offered participants more opportunity to explore feelings. My sense of discontent and inadequacy grew. I also began feeling considerable envy in the presence of therapists who seemed to be doing their work with such ease. It has always seemed to me that every feeling is given for a good purpose and that the function of envy might well be to point out the direction in which one is intended to move. I went back to Lou Ormont to share again my yearning and dissatisfaction. When I had last talked to him about doing group work I was fifty-three and thought myself too old. Now I was fifty-seven. "Am I too old?" I asked again. "Forget about age," Lou said. "There are people who are old at twenty-five and people who are young at eighty-five. Never let age be a deterrent." Then he added, " I do have a new requirement since you were here last. I will accept you into my program only after you have begun work with two groups in Washington and are meeting weekly with the group consultant to whom I will refer you."

"How can I ever manage that?" I responded in utter disbelief. "Have no fear," he said. "You will do it." His words were both supporting and challenging. A program that would have seemed out of my reach up until that moment filled me with the kind of exhilaration the mountain climber must know as he sets out to climb his highest peak.

Looking back on those experiences with Robert Raines, Lou Ormont, and others, I realize that these helpers and guides enabled me to tap hidden resources in myself so that I could do what I was ready to do. This is what the miracle workers of the world always do. They restore faith in ourselves to feed the five thousand and raise the dead. We walk on water because they make us forget that we do not know how.

Small Growth Groups

Each week I am the leader of five growth groups made up of eight to ten persons. Last night at the end of a group session one of the members commented, "Church was good tonight." He put into words what is so often my experience in the small growth group where members gather for the implicit, if not explicit reason of grappling for the truth of their lives and facing into the resistances that impede that struggle.

For me, the small group, or therapy group as it is called in its secular setting, closely resembles the involvement of the twelve together. Jesus gave an occasional hillside sermon, but he spent most of his time in the company of a very few, trudging country roads with them, telling and hearing stories around campfires, listening in on quarrels, and attending to issues around such emotionally charged subjects as money, sex, vocation, competition, and betrayal. His days were given to teaching twelve men how to relate to one another—helping them to take their feelings out of bondage and deal openly with their negative responses to each other. He told them that, if they knew of anyone in the community who had something against them, it was more important to sit down with that person and try to resolve the difference than to be in church worshiping God. He believed that to be insincere with one's feelings brought about loss of soul, and he taught that what one was on the outside had to correspond with what one was on the inside. His dangerous vocation was that of an educator. The disciples in their turn took up that same vocation. The message of Jesus sounded in their teaching, "confess your dark feelings and thoughts and deeds to one another, and pray for one another, and then you will be cured" (James 5:16). I am convinced that the reason we suffer so much and yearn for a deeper experience of community is that we have failed to create the structures that make possible the implementation of this bold New Testament teaching.

The growth group exists to provide members a place in which they will begin to feel safe enough to express thoughts and feelings that in ordinary circumstances they might keep hidden away inside them for fear of offending or alienating others. In a climate of acceptance where we are free to confess what is on our hearts we discover what is true and what is false in ourselves, what is dross and what is gold, what is important for us and what is unimportant—things that are never easy to know. The purpose of work in the group is to become one's true self fully and completely. Christ calls us to this work. It is the vocation to which all other vocations are subordinate. "What will a man gain by winning the whole world, at the cost of his true self? Or what can he give that will buy that self back?" (Matt. 16:26, NEB).

The contract for small group work that I like best is easy to explain though difficult to follow. I learned it while doing group work with Lou Ormont. Dr. Ormont accepted me into his training program because he believed as I do that lay persons could be trained to give leadership to small intentional growth groups. In his writings he spells out the group contract in three provisions, all of which apply to communication:

1. That each member tell his thoughts and feelings toward the other members and why he has them.
2. That each member put into words what he understands about another member.
3. That each member relate the emotionally significant story of his life—past, future, and particularly present.

In addition Dr. Ormont cites four ground rules:

1. That each member attend all sessions and arrive on time.
2. That each member pay his bills on time.
3. That each member refrain from acting-in or acting-out.

4. That each member preserve the confidence of the other members' identities and the information they reveal.[37]

In the course of my work with this doctor of souls I heard one other condition:

5. That each member be responsible for taking his proportionate amount of the group's time.

Dr. Ormont expected and accepted deviations from the contract, which he sometimes pondered in his own heart, but more often brought to the violator's attention. As members of the group we learned from him how to hold each other accountable and to inquire into the reasons for our failures.

The first commandment in Dr. Ormont's covenant—to reveal thoughts and feelings toward other members—is the most difficult to follow. To be faithful to it may mean telling another what one knows she does not want to hear, or more dreaded still, hearing uncomplimentary news about oneself. Sometimes the feelings one needs to confess are those of which one is deeply ashamed, such as "I am envious of you because you can buy whatever you want," or "I am jealous of you because you always have Bill's attention," or "I am angry with you for always interrupting and never finding my thoughts important." At other times the feelings one needs to confess are tender and loving ones. "I feel good when you are around. I am more positive about myself, more able to do what I want to do," or "The way you assume responsibility makes me feel less burdened," or "I have warm feelings toward you. I don't know why. They are just there."

Other members are encouraged to share their responses to the situation. One member may say, "I share your feelings, Doris. John is always interrupting and it makes me angry, too." Another member might add, "My experience of you, John, is quite different. I find you very attentive to my thoughts. I am also tempted to interrupt you, Doris, because you go on and on, not knowing when to stop."

Such exchanges can be painful, and yet they cannot be avoided for it is through our pain and our darkness that we grow. When members look back on their experience in a group they recognize that the times of anger and conflict were also the times of enlightenment and transformation, even though in the moment it did not feel that way. It is one thing to subscribe to a teaching outside us that says the truth will set us free, and another to receive that teaching into the heart where one's whole being will be affected. We can give lip service to the fact that we can not detect our own failings, pray to be cleansed of hidden faults (Ps. 19:12), and still shrink from their uncovering.

Most of us would rather go through life nursing the secret grudge, keeping our distance from one another, hanging on to feelings of hurt, distrust, and suspicion rather than bringing them into the light where a healing process can begin. Even with a group that has a covenant to do this, the task is extraordinarily difficult. Unless we have something pleasant to say we are afraid that the other will not hear us. In fact, if we say how things really are with us, we fully suspect that the other will turn away. This conviction is not unrelated to reality. Each of us has a storehouse of pain from the times when we failed in trying to communicate feelings and perceptions that were important to us, or succeeded and found that what we thought and felt was not allowed by others. We will probably always feel that an effort to reveal the deeper self is risky, which may be why the Scriptures say that salvation is to be worked out in fear and trembling.

With any deep revelation of ourselves we will have a feeling of nakedness and the vulnerability and shame that go with nakedness. These may be the reasons shame has been called the truly revolutionary feeling.

When there is no one to listen to our sorrows we begin stockpiling them in our own hearts so that, even when a delayed invitation to give them a hearing is extended, we are afraid lest they overwhelm us. The fear is not ungrounded. Feelings deterred from natural expression, denied and repressed, take up existence outside our control where they continue to gather energy. In a matter of time that energy will burst its bonds and be used against ourselves and others. Take, for example, the emotion of anger. Behind anger is always a feeling of hurt, of having been treated unfairly. It begs a hearing.

I am quite sure that anger motivates us to address perceived injustice toward ourselves and injustice toward others, and yet we have made anger one of the forbidden emotions. At the same time, we deplore iniquity in the world as though that world existed on its own and did not reflect what was going on in our hearts. An emotion meant to be used for reconciliation and the creating of a just order is imprisoned in our lives where it claws at our stomachs and embitters our hearts, causing us all kinds of physical and psychic pain.

The potentially destructive element in stored-up anger has added to our fear of it. Rather than acknowledge that this fiery emotion is part of our own experience, we keep it wetted down with our tears, and hidden behind gracious smiles. In the polite society of our churches we find it difficult to tolerate any expression of anger in ourselves or in others, even when it may be the appropriate response. This is not to say that anger is always appropriate, but how do we discover whether it is or not unless we let another know that we are angry? Communication of feeling like the communication of thought can be learned. Feelings like thoughts can be understood. To be sure when too long contained, they will burst their bonds and be used to attack. Thus the plea to learn to use anger creatively to set things right.

William Blake in his poem "The Poison Tree" says eloquently what I am struggling to say:

> I was angry with my friend:
> I told my wrath, my wrath did end.
> I was angry with my foe:
> I told it not, my wrath did grow.
>
> And I water'd it in fears,
> Night & morning with my tears;

And I sunned it with smiles,
And with soft deceitful wiles.

And it grew both day and night,
Till it bore an apple bright.
And my foe beheld it shine,
And he knew that it was mine.

And into my garden stole,
When the night had veil'd the pole;
In the morning glad I see,
My foe outstretch'd beneath the tree.[38]

Few of us know that a person telling his anger is a person in the process of getting over anger. The person who is angry and not verbally expressing that anger is the person from whom we have more to fear. Such is the anger erupting in families and on battlefields. The terrorist acts in our homes are giving way more and more to crazed terrorist acts in streets and skies.

Most of us in the churches will seek to save our relationships with each other by not expressing the anger we feel when we are neglected, rejected, or misused. All unbeknownst to us a distancing begins. In our undeclared hearts will grow feelings of alienation and loneliness, a yearning for intimacy. Rarely in our relationships do we have the experience, so common to small groups who work with feelings, of seeing the pain that is behind anger, or of discovering in ourselves warmth and closeness for the person toward whom we were able to share our hurt feelings or negative thoughts. In fact, those feelings of closeness are in their turn so rarely expressed that few of us have the opportunity of knowing that anger, listened to and addressed, gives way to warmth and trust. Even when the other fails to understand the reason for one's grieving, the anger is still diminished by the simple expression of it. Speech is a very great power with extraordinary healing properties. Sigmund Freud discovered this in listening to people, and described psychoanalysis as the "talking cure." We are healed when we can take what is inside us and place it outside us where we can look at it and gain the perspective that is needed to make good choices.

Our difficulty in knowing our feelings is caused by living in a society that teaches us to wear masks, to pretend to have feelings that we do not have, to be ashamed of our human nature, to hide our true selves. In time we come to believe the lie we tell to others, and a lie, in the words of William Blake, is "the negation of passion." To the extent that we have had to repress and suppress feelings, our capacity to feel atrophies. Our lives are either volcanoes waiting to explode or, more likely, frozen ponds where everything fiery in us has been put on ice. We feel lukewarm or cold inside, if not numb and dead. Our staggering task is to recover our passion, to steal back the fire of which we have been robbed. To be sure, fire can rage out of control, but it also can be contained within a burning bush or a burning coal.

> Then one of the seraphim flew to me carrying in his hand a burning coal which he had taken from the altar with a pair of tongs. He touched my mouth with it and said,
> See, this has touched your lips;
> your iniquity is removed,
> and your sin is wiped away.
> Isaiah 6:6-7, NEB

Matthew Fox states that compassion in our age has gone into exile, and surely he is right. The proper response, however, is not to shake our heads and exhort each other to pity and good works. What is required is more mercy, not more judgment and exhortation. According to Webster, passion means any one of the emotions—hate, grief, love, fear, joy, anger, rage, fury. How can we have compassion—feel with another—when we have refused to keep company with our own woeful feelings? Every banished feeling will set up its own oppressive regime. Anger cannot be exiled without dragging love along with it; the same is true of all the emotions. We cannot be selective and outlaw the less presentable ones. Each walks hand in hand with its opposite.

The rich complexity of our emotional life is another sign of God's creativity. If that is indeed so, then every feeling is meant to serve us. Each has a place in God's design. Each is needed for wholeness. When I consider any part of the body—the hands, the feet, the mouth, the ears—I have some comprehension of how wondrously we are wrought, and that no part, not even one little toe, can be easily given up. The same is true of that great range of emotions, all of which will be constellated in us, if we live our lives fully in community with one another.

I yearn for the gift of Paul that I might as vividly set forth the indispensability of any one of our feelings in the way that he was able to do for the various parts of the body:

> . . . God put all the separate parts into the body on purpose. If all the parts were the same, how could it be a body? As it is, the parts are many but the body is one. The eye cannot say to the hand, "I do not need you," nor can the head say to the feet, "I do not need you" (1 Cor. 12:18–21).

Each of our feelings is as urgently needed as each one of the parts of our bodies. The suppression of any one of them diminishes us. We may not know the purpose of our negative emotions because we have not allowed ourselves to put them into words, to feel them, and to explore them. We have so censored them in the church that confession of them has become too wounding to an already damaged self-esteem. When our pain becomes too great we are driven outside the church to find the "priests" who will help us know why we suffer. The difficulty is that these priests are not enough in number, nor do they have the slightest intention of ministering to the suffering masses in our inner cities and country towns. The church, having handed over to a few high-priced professionals its listening vocation, has no greater task in our age than the regaining of that vocation. Life on this planet may be dependent on it.

When negative feelings do not find expression and have not become reconciled with their opposites, the human frame is miserably torn and afflicted. What is suppressed and repressed in us corrupts our hearts and makes them into repositories of evil. The darkness we cannot own and explore in ourselves wreaks havoc in our relationships and havoc in the world, as we are seeing every day. As all healers tell us, we cannot attain a high degree of consciousness until we discover in ourselves that which corresponds to what we are judging in others. Most of us will not be able to do that work without someone who will seriously listen to us, and in today's world there are very few who can give that essential help.

The ministry of listening is learned by listening to one's own deeper being, which means opening oneself to the pain in unwanted thoughts and feelings. We usually try to avoid or deaden emotional pain rather than get at the issues it is intended to bring to our attention. In all creation the capacity to know pain has been given only to animals and, more abundantly, to humans. Pain is the hallmark of our humanity—an awesome fact.

Negative emotions always carry the experience of pain when we allow ourselves to feel them. Envy, jealousy, greed, anger, lust, never feel good and in their extreme each carries its own peculiar agony. They are all cries of pain that plead for attention as discomfort in the body seeks to alert and arouse us to discover an illness. A painful emotion tries to give us a message, to tell us something needs to be done if we are to feel well again. Perhaps we have wandered into an environment that is not in tune with our inmost self; or the time may have come to strike out in a new direction; or perhaps an ignored potential in us will not be kept in wraps any longer.

Could it be that envy signals hidden treasure? Do we envy in another the gift that is latent in our own beings? If we could acknowledge our envy perhaps we might find in ourselves the buried talent.

And what of jealousy? Scripture seems to indicate that its purpose is to stir us to good works. Paul suggests this when, in his letter to the Romans, he tells them that he was sent to the pagans in order to make his own people jealous and in that way to save some of them (Rom. 11:14, NEB). Moses before him said, "I will make you jealous of people who are not even a nation; I will make you angry with an irreligious people" (Rom. 10:19).

<u>And who will say a good word for greed?</u> I will, my Lord. My <u>guess is that if we were willing to feel its pain deep down, we</u> <u>would discover how empty our souls are, how very great is our</u> <u>inner poverty.</u> Instead, greed is condemned in sermons and exalted in practice. If we could experience greed's pain, we might go in search of imperishable bread for the poor in ourselves. Then we would be able to make *real* friends with the poor in our communities and the poor in the world. These are groups that need each other—the poor in us, the poor around us, and the poor in the world. Together these three groups would be a great force for change—sufficient reason for the powerful in the world to encourage enmity between and among them.

Is lust an attempt to recover through another one's own lost sense of self-worth, or does it signal a thwarted desire to love and to create? Alfred Kazin, in an introduction to his selection of writings by William Blake, emphasized that Blake's Jesus is a friend of man's desire, "which is never vicious in itself; it is only turned to vicious ends when driven out of its real channel."[39]

We cannot have a rich inner life or a priestly vocation without understanding and educating our feelings. Our feelings make up our emotional life and determine whether it is healthy or not healthy. The emotions also determine how we act, and whether we act in and upon the world. Our emotions are what move us and what enable us to move others.

Emotion has its root in the French *emouvoir*, to stir up, and the Latin *exmovere*, to move. We want our emotions to be able to stir us up. This does not mean that all of our feelings are appropriate. If that were true, feelings at an immature stage of development would not impose the immense threat that they do in the modern world. Our feelings like our thoughts can be based on what is unreal. We must, nonetheless, learn to feel for ourselves just as we must learn to think for ourselves, even though it means taking the risk of going off the deep end and falling into an abyss. When we do not nurture growth in our emotional life, we leave our feelings at an arrested stage. We do not grow up, but remain immature, if not infantile, in our response to life.

Columbus could not know that the world was round. A trained and disciplined mind told him that it was, and he had to act on that assumption. Had he been in error, he would probably have discovered it before he took a ship, its crew, and himself over the edge. In the same way we must train and discipline our feelings, and then find the courage to act upon them. If our feelings are based on a mistaken sense of reality, we have more chance of discovering their falsity before being wrecked by them. In any case we have to take that chance. Failure to close the gap between emotional and intellectual development puts us each day in risk of world catastrophe.

The time will surely come when no one will be elected to high office in any land without spending at least three years in some kind of therapy program. In a nuclear age, however, every leader and each of his advisers need, in addition, a continuing group where feelings and thoughts can be processed— where there is time for reflection and mulling over matters of the heart.

As things are now, governments have made self-examination a sign of weakness rather than of strength and nobility of soul. When a public figure does seek self-knowledge or the cause of his suffering he runs the risk of becoming a pariah, barred from holding official positions. Those who take the risk have reminded me of Nicodemus going to Jesus by night, hoping that his visit will not be made known. As a result of this kind of oppression, the affairs of government are conducted out of the unconscious. The lack of opportunity to develop a feeling mind and a thinking heart brings about a dearth of imagination and vision in the world. As for the churches . . . we find there no burning bushes or angels of annunciation to arrest our attention.

The matter of giving too little attention to emotional gifts is actually more serious for the church, since this is the institution charged with the development of the whole person. What other institution has the daring to speak of metanoia and transformation—the new being? At the same time our most distinguished writers and theologians let slip from their pens and their tongues words that denigrate any conscious pursuit of self-knowledge, and are all unaware that this is what they are doing. Instead of giving the leadership that would encourage people to use all the help available to them in becoming emotionally awake, they sometimes make disparaging remarks about people who sit around in small groups "endlessly looking into each others' psyches." Although they are intellectual giants and guides, they have little *emotional* understanding that the feelings that we are aware of and become responsible for are the ones that release us from self and send us into the world.

Christianity states that the truth will make us free, but leaves us to discover the ways we feed our illusions and lie to others and to ourselves. We are told not to let the sun set upon our anger, thus giving us the monumental task of learning to use anger creatively so that it is not stored up in our systems, condemning us to years of rage and hostility. We are told to honor father and mother, which means that we must come to see them as struggling human beings like ourselves, worthy of forgiveness.

We are to be brothers and sisters to each other, but what about the sibling rivalry and jealousy that we cannot put aside? How do we take the plank out of our own eye? When we give our attention to these concerns we are being faithful. We are not always able to discern God's will for our lives, but in pursuing matters of the heart, we do not have to be plagued with uncertainty. Only a pseudo-Christianity makes a distinction between spirituality and the inward journey of knowing oneself. Knowing oneself and knowing God are not two separate things. They are a seamless robe, one intricately bound with the other.

For the simple reason that we have given so little attention to the education of our feelings, the small group is a safer place than the world to discover what is true in our hearts and what is false—to begin to understand that our counsel to a friend might be based on jealousy rather than concern for the friend; that our graciousness may cloak envy; that our anger is out of proportion to an event; that our love may hide a morbid dependency; and that what feels like virtue to us sounds like self-righteousness to another.

In a group that develops the coherence and trust that enable and encourage members to risk self-disclosure and to give to one another honest feedback, change takes place for the simple reason that participants are free to explore their fears around vocational choice, concerns about inadequacy and low self-esteem, strivings after perfection and the approval of others, dependency needs, intimacy, and a host of other issues. They can explore reactions of envy, jealousy, competitiveness, sex, and greed, and not feel isolated. In a group there is usually more than one person to say, "I know how that must feel because of this and this in me." What we discover in the small growth group is that we are all pilgrims with the same common earth beneath our feet or, as a friend liked to say at crucial moments in the life of her group, "We are all bozos on this bus together."

The small growth group is a structure for becoming aware of what is happening inside us and of opening ourselves to transformation. By letting others know what feels good to us and what feels bad we learn to communicate in constructive and compassionate ways. The small group with its hard but life-giving covenant becomes the place of self-revelation and discovery, for the admitting into consciousness the questions we did not know we had, for learning to be curious about ourselves because others are curious about us. The experience is one of acceptance, forgiveness, communion—a glimpse into the mystery of redemption, of holiness. "Church was good tonight."

24

Learnings from an Illness

For more than twenty months I had been unable to make the effort to sit at my typewriter. Arthritis, the illness that plagued my childhood and early youth, had struck with force once again. All I could manage were scribbled notes on the experience of being ill. Now that I am well I want to write of it more fully.

As a way of coping I became a student of the disease that plagued me. My attention was focused on it in a way that might be called self-absorbed were it not for the fact that when one is ill the illness becomes one's work. When we ask a patient how he feels we are asking him to talk about his work. Patients need to remember, however, that as vital as that work is, few persons have any tolerance for hearing about it and are of little comfort in the battle with depression that is a part of any long illness. Our friends for the most part enjoy us when we are well, and feel deprived when we are ill. Responses ranged all the way from anger and disbelief to warmth and compassion. I learned to cherish as special messengers those who companioned me on this journey. They proved true the words of Simone Weil, "The love of our neighbor in all its fullness simply means being able to say . . . What are you going through?"[40]

To the extent that we are wounded in our bodies the spirit also falls ill. No wonder Satan chided God that his testing of the faithful Job had failed to lay a finger on his bone and flesh. Our relationship with our bodies is the most intimate one we have in this world, but one we often fail to recognize until physical pain reminds us that we are forever locked in an interdependent relationship. The spirit, the personality, the intelligence, the I AM in each of us has been given one house to live in, to be relinquished only at death.

My body and I serve or fail to serve each other to the enhancement or diminishment of each. My body is my only constant companion, and though I may fall into a slave-master relationship with it, this is not my intention. I respect too much the intricate relationship between us. In fact, I believe that my particular body is especially adept in registering my psychic conflicts and my failure to listen to my inmost self. Of course, in the very same way my emotional life can be a reflection of what is happening in my body.

Our bodies as well as the events of every day teach us the lesson that "life is not fair." One body is given to its owner tragically flawed at birth, while another carries its tenant soul gracefully into old age. Fairness and equality are not in the natural order of things, though our beings have been coded to protest unfairness. If the scales that justice holds do not seem to balance, we ask ourselves, "Can it be that I have sinned?" or the even more dreaded question, "Does the Almighty pervert justice?" (Job 8:3, NEB).

In a period of discouragement, I struggled with these questions and pondered some of the literature on illness. Norman Cousins in his book, *Anatomy of an Illness*, summed up for me many of the feelings I had experienced through the months when my illness was most acute:

> There was first of all the feeling of helplessness—a serious disease in itself.
>
> There was the subconscious fear of never being able to function normally again—and it produced a wall of separation between us and the world of open movement, open sounds, open expectations.
>
> There was the reluctance to be thought a complainer.
>
> There was the desire not to add to the already great burden of apprehension felt by one's family; this added to the isolation.
>
> There was the conflict between the terror of loneliness and the desire to be left alone.
>
> There was the lack of self-esteem, the subconscious feeling perhaps that our illness was a manifestation of our inadequacy.

There was the fear that decisions were being made behind our backs, that not everything was made known that we wanted to know, yet dreaded knowing.

There was the morbid fear of intrusive technology, fear of being metabolized by a data base, never to regain our faces again. There was resentment of strangers who came to us with needles and vials—some of which put supposedly magic substances in our veins, and others which took more of our blood than we thought we could afford to lose. There was the distress of being wheeled through white corridors to laboratories for all sorts of strange encounters with compact machines and blinking lights and whirling discs.

And there was the utter void created by the longing— ineradicable, unremitting, pervasive—for warmth of human contact. A warm smile and an outstretched hand were valued even above the offerings of modern science, but the latter were far more accessible than the former.[41]

Though my most recent experience with illness did not include any sojourn in a hospital and was never life-threatening, at one time or another I felt most of the above. The disease which raged in my limbs and stole my energy also made me open to anything that might make me well, an attitude that is one of the primary gifts of pain. It unlocks our closed world. While that same openness may make sufferers the easy prey of charlatans, on the other hand it makes them willing to listen to the possibilities in therapeutic methods that present viable alternatives to drugs. When we are well and have what we need for comfort, the tendency is to be closed and conservative. Finding risk unnecessary, we cling to what we have. As the autobiographies of too many doctors tell us, not until they themselves became ill did they understand how inadequate was the training that made them treat only the patient's disease— not the patient.

For the first four weeks I was convinced that my illness would run its course as it had so many times in years gone by. In those weeks it seemed to me that I had a two-fold task: one, to provide for my body the optimum conditions for recovery so that a damaged immune system might be restored. For me this meant rest, good food, peaceful thoughts, and all the exercise I could manage, which for months was to be only a bare minimum. The second task was to try to understand what had triggered in me the disease that had been absent or dormant and which I had come to think had departed forever. Was it the stress of a burned-out office, or, as allergists suggested, the strong smell of paint and chemically treated carpet that had afterwards permeated the room for weeks; or too much coffee and too long hours over too long a time, or had something burned out in me? Had I for too long been giving more than I was receiving; or, more likely still, was it the growing tension between conflicting claims? I wanted to begin the new work of bringing into being Sarah's Circle; I wanted to continue my work as a group therapist; I wanted to crawl away into a lonely place and write the book that was stirring inside my life—all of these could not be satisfied at once, which was what I wanted. There are other kinds of greed than the greed for money.

I was never to find a certain answer to the cause of my illness. Any one of the above could have triggered the virulent assault, or perhaps they had all combined forces to activate a dormant virus. In any case more than my body was ailing. I wanted a wholistic approach to healing my body, mind, and spirit which had fallen into disease.

For weeks I resisted professional friends who assured me that new drugs were on the market, and that they would have me back on my feet in no time. I felt I might miss the meaning of this illness for my life—the message for the future of which I am quite sure every illness is the bearer—and be forever dependent on drugs rather than facing what needed to be changed in me. Equally important were the mounds of literature I read those first weeks which alerted me to the fact that, while these wonder drugs have the potential of relieving the symptoms, they have no curative value and each has the potential of moderate to serious adverse effects. I was afraid not to give my body the chance to heal itself. Something or someone was instructing me that there are times when we must be willing to wait for health and a feeling of well-being, a difficult thing to do in a drug-addicted culture. The hard, statistical evidence is that arthritis, for all the promise of the new drugs, remains the number one crippler of children and adults.

I knew my disease was not the trivial aches and pains of old age, but a serious and formidable adversary that threatened my whole way of life. I did not want to trust too quickly in promises too easily made. Fortifying me in my position was harsh experience. I had seen the effects of medicines overprescribed for people I knew well. More than this, years ago I had agreed to everything "learned doctors" prescribed for Richard, my twin brother, who had come home from World War II with his heart and mind in confusion. First, the most prestigious treatment center in one metropolitan area said Richard's future depended on his taking a series of eight deep insulin shock treatments—since called the "savage sleep." When he sank deeper into himself, they recommended more insulin shock until the treatments reached fifty. The next doctors prescribed a series of electric shock treatments which they assured me had been found effective when used in conjunction with insulin, and which, they insisted, must be started immediately. When that series of twenty-four treatments was finished, the patient was forever lost to himself and to those who cared about him except for a smile which now and then breaks through from hidden places to remind us of ties not completely severed.

What we did not know then was that overdoses of insulin resulted in a dangerous and convulsive state of unconsciousness, albeit a treatment intended to cure. Electric shock, still controversial today, is used in much smaller dosages and only after careful and specific diagnoses. What happened in that not so-long-ago period can be judged only as wild and reckless use of untested procedures. The doctors prescribing those treatments pressured families to consent to them, as though all the evidence were in. Their cold and authoritative tones forbade questioning. No reservations clouded the conclusive finality of their recommendations. The risk was all placed on delay.

That was the heyday of shock treatment. The pages in medical history that followed were as tragic and even more grim— the lobotomy era, pioneered in the hospitals of this country by surgeons holding all the credentials that inspire trust. Between 1943 and 1951 thousands of mental patients were subjected to the psychosurgeon's knife in the hope of ending, or at least reducing, overcrowding on mental wards. We were called into the hospital where Richard was and informed of how promising the simple operation would be for him. When we refused to give permission, a doctor told us that our uncooperativeness was not in the patient's interest. "We are disappointed," he said. "We wish you would think about it and call us."

In the beginning the operation was used only on patients who had not improved within six months of confinement. Later its most renowned advocate was to say, "It is safer to operate than to wait."

Newspaper accounts from that disturbing era indicate that the drive for lobotomies was fueled by understaffed and overcrowded hospitals. The debate on the scandalous experiment was brought to an end by the advent of tranquilizers which came along to subdue patients. While these powerful drugs do not help every mental patient, they offer hope to many. Early pilot projects demonstrated that drug therapy used in conjunction with support programs would enable as many as 60 percent of mental patients to become productive members of society.

The recommended "therapeutic centers" and community-based programs, however, were never put in place. Another bizarre chapter was added to medical and legal history—the cruel dumping of mental patients onto communities totally unprepared to help them. More than half of the nation's homeless are thought to be the victims of a program of "deinstitutionalization" that is failing for lack of attention to housing and essential support services. Though clinically and morally wrong, each day more and more mental patients are put out on urban streets to forage and fend for themselves as best they can. They are innocents, and yet this new crime against them is never named a crime, and may not even be thought of as such. In a future, more civilized day, it will be ranked with slavery and other terrible outrages against humanity that could not happen except for the indifference of those who are not personally touched.

These dark chapters in the care of the mentally ill, together with other experiences, helped to make me the so-called "difficult patient." Over the years doctors and experts lost the mystique with which I had surrounded them. They became faulted human beings like us all, with their own biases, prejudices, and limitations.

Today, to qualify as my doctor, a physician must indicate by gesture or word that I am an esteemed consultant and partner in my body's healing process. Despite the physician's years of study and practice, there is an experience that only I know— the one of being inside the body that is the patient. My body is unlike any other body, as surely as my fingerprint is unlike every other fingerprint. It must have its own inner shaman proclaiming as best it can what it needs for healing. I am the only one privy to that counsel. I am also the one that will bear the consequences of inappropriate treatment.

As strong as these convictions were they did not enable me to maintain control over my life. After I had been ill for over a month with no abatement in the disease, I went to see a rheumatologist who, before I grasped what was happening, had injected steroids into my knees, a procedure that is considered by many doctors as one of last resort. The problem is that doctor and patient are not evenly matched when it comes to a contest of wills. He was well and I was sick; he was standing up, I was lying down; he was fully clothed and I was draped in an inadequate paper gown; he said he knew what was best, I could make no such claim; I was alone in his setting, he was flanked by his nurse and walls that held framed certificates of his achievements; I was anxious and he was angry. "The only other treatment," he said, "is prayer and I don't pray." He won when he should have lost.

It took me several weeks to extricate myself from this doctor and his program, and to find Dr. Patience White, the wise and gentle head of rheumatology at George Washington Hospital. After reviewing my medical history, Dr. White advised a conservative approach, which I was glad to follow, although I believe I would have trusted myself to any treatment she recommended. Faith, so essential to the healing process, was back in my life. I wonder whether anyone ever gets well when this ingredient is missing.

Alma Newitt came to pray for me during those weeks and, at her urging, on a Wednesday night I went to a prayer service that Francis McNutt held at Wesley Seminary. After his talk he invited anyone who wanted special prayer to come forward for a laying on of hands. The aisles began to fill. Unable to stand long enough to be in the procession I stayed at the back of the church with my legs stretched out in the pew. It was healing just to watch from there the scene of faith being enacted in that sanctuary. When the last petitioner had returned to his seat we were all invited to hold hands for a corporate prayer. I did not see the solitary figure in the pew behind me until he tapped me on the shoulder and, holding out his hand, whispered, "I need your strength." Meeting the fear in his eyes with the fear in mine I took his hand and felt for the first time a part of that community of believers. Until that time I had not known that they needed anything from me. The words of a man I had never seen before and would never see again will always stay with me: "I need your strength." They spoke to me of our dependence on one another. ". . . so all of us, in union with Christ, form one body, and as parts of it we belong to each other" (Rom. 12:4). Drawn as I am to contemplative prayer, I had not attended many prayer meetings or healing services, but, in this area also, pain had given me an openness.

In the days that followed I read the healing stories in the Gospel of Matthew. I especially pondered the one of the lame man whose friends had broken through a neighbor's roof to place him in the way of Jesus' healing power. Alma did this for me. Her faith in prayer was of a different kind than my own. She did what she could to put me in the company of those who she felt were special channels of God's healing, and so it was that on a summer day I found myself at a prayer service being held in a small house in Virginia.

After the Bible study, the leader, a humble and simple woman of faith, who kept herself out of the way of her message, prayed for each person who went forward, placing her hands on the petitioner's head. Her prayers were long, but direct and specific. She prayed that I might be willing to give up rowing my own boat and turn the oars over to God—to relax and to trust. As she prayed I became aware of a wind blowing on me. I thought it was a fan and was distracted by it. Vulnerable to drafts, I felt uncomfortable as it blew upon me. Then it seemed as though it might be the heavy breathing of the woman praying. I turned my face away from her, but that breath felt strong on my face. When her prayer was over and I returned to my seat I searched the room for a fan. There was none. As I watched her pray for the next person who seated himself before her I could see that he was well out of the range of her breath. The words of an old hymn said, "Breathe on me, breath of God." Christ had breathed on his disciples. I had thought that this was the imagery of poets.

In the months to come my disability continued to make me open to anything that promised health. I tried a number of diets that had been helpful to others. They did not cure me, but I made discoveries that brought me closer to the poor of the world and closer to the earth. I feel best now when I am eating whole grains, beans, and vegetables—the foods that were once the staples of our own poor people before they were lured from them by the inferior and expensive offerings of fast food chains. *Diet for a Small Planet*[42] made me grieve for the children of our inner cities who shun meals of rice, beans, and kale for hamburgers, French fries, and Coke.

At about this time, Norman Cousins called at the request of a mutual friend. He asked me the germane questions that no doctor had asked.

Did I feel my creativity was blocked? Did I have any long-standing resentments or frustrations? "The main task," he said, "is to get the abuse out of your life whether it is from drugs or people."

He asked me what I had eaten for breakfast, for lunch, and what I planned to eat for supper. What had I eaten for these three meals the day before? He then gave me a recipe for a salad since I had made no mention of one: chopped cabbage, green pepper, radish, bean sprouts, broccoli, and all kinds of lettuce. He also gave me the titles of several books on relaxation.

When I thought the conversation was about to end my mentor led me through a twenty-minute meditation which began with the instruction to remember the time in my life when I was happiest. I could hardly follow him in the guided tour of this segment of my life for remembering that the man on the other end of the line was Norman Cousins, the writer whose thinking over many years had so often quickened my mind and heart. He ended his call with an assignment: I was to identify my brand of humor, and note each week three things that had absolutely delighted me. Finally, in an immensely generous act, he gave to the stranger on the other end of the telephone his number at home and at work, and invited me to call and let him know how I was doing.

If a telephone call could make one well that call would have done it. It was an alabaster jar of oil poured over my head, teaching me something about how to doctor and how to pastor.

As it was, however, my recovery took place very gradually over a two-year period with many ups and downs. I could not credit any one thing with restoring my health, which is just as well since I, too, tend to absolutize the way that helps me and to believe that it will be helpful to everyone else. Whoever the agent may be, the healer is God, and he seems to like variety and to exercise considerable imagination. One day he used the stirred waters of a pool for healing, and on another he made a paste with earth and spittle and anointed the eyes of a blind man.

When we are well it is easier to be prosaic and to endorse only the scientific. Sufferers are the ones who know that mud and chants may be involved in their healing, information that can hardly be appreciated before we ourselves are beset with calamity. When the renowned and influential scientist Margaret Mead lay dying in one of Manhattan's famed centers of medicine, she sent for a Chilean faith healer to touch and massage the diseased areas of her body. Boyce Rensberger, reporting in *Science* magazine on this last phase of her journey, wrote that Mead considered this healer the modern equivalent of the shamans and witch doctors that she had known in so many traditional cultures. "After 53 years studying exotic rituals and strange ways of thinking, Mead was turning her skills as a 'participant observer' to the ultimate human act, her own final rite of passage." Rensberger reports that her close friend, Wilton Dillon, an official of the Smithsonian Institute and one of the pilgrims at her bedside, said that some of Mead's friends were afraid her scientific reputation would be damaged if it got out that she was consulting a faith healer. "There are people who didn't want this known publicly," Dillon said, "but I think it was a case of Margaret being willing to tolerate any source, information, or help."[43]

I value the insights, technology, and drugs of modern science. I would not want to be without them. I argue no return to olden days, though I am sure an archetype of a medicine man or witch doctor dwells in me and that I sometimes sound like one or the other. The reputed intuitiveness and sensitivity to the numinous of ancient healers are what attract me. These are qualities I try to nurture and trust in myself, and gravitate toward in others.

More than this, in an age of experts I want to be expert in being responsible for my own life. I was late in learning that this is a primary obligation. Old habits of dependency are hard to break, so I say often that we cannot give to another authority over our body, mind, or heart. Our doctors and guides are also persons in pain. They speak out of their own experiences, biases, and faulted understanding as we each do. We must listen well to them, and then take counsel with ourselves.

I bless Yahweh, who is my counsellor,
and in the night my inmost self instructs me.

Psalm 16:7

All illnesses—spiritual, emotional, or physical—require a wholistic program of treatment. The person who makes you laugh and take heart is not likely to be the same person who can tell you what your medical options are, or the one who can tell you which foods have the potential of healing you, or the one who can help you to pray.

In my own months of illness my best counsel on prayer came in a chance conversation with a friend who told me that in a time of bad depression he had been helped by the practice of giving praise for everything including his depression. My parched heart drank in his words, which may be sign enough that they were pointing me in the right direction. I had considered adopting a discipline of praise a dozen years before when I had read the book, *Power in Praise* by Merlin Carothers.[44] Though the book is poorly written, the author's message is forceful and compelling. Even so it made no real claim on me, and I did not think about it again until Richard Baer came to visit and left me a paper in which he recounted how he had been irresistibly drawn by Carothers' earlier book, *Prison to Praise.*[45] Despite his first reservations, Baer came to feel that it was an extraordinary book. He summed up Carothers' message in these words:

One can learn to think and praise God not only for the good things in life—the joys and delights and blessings—but one can and should also praise God for pain and difficulty, for problems and adversity, for the dark and destructive things in our lives. It is not just that we should praise God in the midst of these circumstances. That would not have been particularly new to me and in no way theologically problematical. Rather we should praise God *for* the pain and the problems. If you are an alcoholic who has been unable to find deliverance, thank God for this. If your son or daughter has become addicted to heroin, praise God for this and believe that he is going to use even this great evil to work out his own purposes in their lives and in your own. If there are habits and character traits in your life which frustrate you, thank God for them. If there are things in the lives of those close to you which you have tried in vain to accept, perhaps a bad temper, a critical spirit, overeating, perennial lateness, thank God for these things.

As Baer practiced the discipline of giving praise for all things he noted a profound change in himself. Where there had been bitterness and resentment, there was peace; where he had been critical, he felt accepting; even where his outward circumstances remained the same, his attitude toward those circumstances perceptibly changed.

Again, I was caught by the message though I made no real effort to incorporate praise into my life. My rational and scientific self could not agree to suspend reasoning and thank God for the bad. Over the years a person here and there would remind me of the absurd practice of praising God for everything as did a friend whose seven-year-old son was killed when a truck backed over him. Still in depression a year after the child's death, she remembered Carothers' injunction to give praise for all things and began to give praise for the child's life and the child's death and for the pain within her. She did not try to deny her feelings. She owned her suffering and gave praise for it. Within a few weeks the heaviness in her lifted. About that time I began to note that the people who had least reason to give praise were those most seriously open to a conscious practice of it. They were the cloud of witnesses that surrounded me when my turn came to accept as a discipline the practice of giving praise for all things.

I began to experience changes in my life as those before me had noted changes in theirs. I had always felt that my prayers lacked sufficient gratitude. That awareness, however, was never forceful enough to prompt in me any focused attention. I was probably most conscious of it when others said grace at table. If I credited God with filling my plate how could I account for empty plates? In a world where children were starving, prayers of thanksgiving for tables groaning with too much food always raised a question in me. If God was the giver, was he not also the withholder?

As I conscientiously praised God for what was hard to bear in my life, I discovered that praise for the good became spontaneous. I could not hold it back. Old theological questions receded into the background altogether. Slowly my whole being came more awake. The quality of my seeing was different. Ordinary things like trees, telephone lines, and tap water filled me with wonder. With a heightened awareness of the created order I also gained a degree of detachment from my body. It became easier to live with uncertainty and to take a long view of the future. I stopped giving undue significance to day-to-day symptoms. I was no longer so sure that I knew what was good and what was bad. Looking back on my life I saw that some things which had seemed so promising at the time later turned out to be disastrous, and some that had felt terrible had turned out to be good. In special moments it was even evident to me that pain and joy were all of a piece. They were separate, but one. Each was the bearer of the other.

In time, my praise began to include my shortcomings—all the lacks in my disposition. I found myself giving praise for me— not as I might hope to be in some distant day, but as I was in the present moment with all my inconsistencies, complaints, impatience, failures at love and forgiveness. For the first time I understood what it was to be acceptable though unacceptable. Praise for my damaged self expanded to include praise for friends and then for the enemies of my peace—those who seemed to be seeking my life, chipping away at it in little ways so that I hardly noticed spirit going out of me. I found strength to "hold to the difficult" as Rilke had counseled:

> How should we be able to forget those ancient myths that are at the beginning of all peoples, the myths about dragons that at the last moment turn into princesses; perhaps all the dragons of our lives are princesses who are only waiting to see us once beautiful

and brave. Perhaps everything terrible is in its deepest being something helpless that wants help from us.[46]

As the experience of life as gift grew steadily stronger in me I became more aware of how dependent each of us is. It seemed as though I had just learned independence, how alone we are, and how little anyone is able to help, when my praise instructed me in how utterly dependent we are. Independence—responsibility for one's self, standing on one's own two feet—met its opposite, dependence. Once again the lion and the lamb in me approached each other and lay down together. I saw how He who had made one had also made the other. We are all creators and givers, but also from the beginning of our days to the end we are beneficiaries, utterly dependent on the love and gifts of others. There is no such thing as a self-made or self-sufficient man or woman. We need each other. That fact loomed larger than it ever had before, and seemed to make the world more precarious than it had been.

Of course, we never really fool ourselves about our vulnerability and dependence on love. In more unconscious times we simply keep the knowledge of it far out of sight where it nonetheless can cause a trembling in us that is hard to define. We know only that we feel unsafe, easy targets for money-changers and counselors with their plans for securing our future in this world and the future of those we care about.

As praise became more a part of my days I moved into a fuller understanding of how very vulnerable every one of us is. At the same time an unseen world swung into sharper focus. I began to feel safer than I had felt before, more able to give shelter to frightening feelings of inadequacy and helplessness. For the first time I understood the meaning of God's becoming vulnerable in Jesus Christ. I wanted to protect his life in me and among us. I even entertained the thought that I might choose to make myself as vulnerable in the world as he had made himself. As I moved closer to the pain inside me, I found myself wanting to be closer to the pain outside me.

In time I began to think what I would do with my life if I were ever well again. I knew I wanted to be a writer once more— perhaps a full-time writer. I had always lacked the courage for so arduous a calling, but now it loomed as a possibility. This meant that I would not return to group work, or try to build Sarah's Circle. With that thought the conflicting claims of different calls once more battled within me.

I could not put Sarah's Circle aside. I wanted to do it for Richard, and I wanted to do it for myself, and for God. I knew of no other way to protect love in myself. I had looked on too much misery not to leave this world in some small way better than I had found it. I believe this is what our suffering requires of us. Others might write about the desperate straits of the mentally ill, the homeless, and the elderly poor. I wanted to find a way to walk among them, to help God breathe on them.

More than any other illness this one had made me feel sad and alone. For months I was not able to sit at a typewriter, or clean my apartment. When I walked in the street it was the walk of a very old woman. In their conversations some of my close friends kept their distance, so little do any of us know about giving and receiving comfort.

My rooms with their French doors gave me a view of sky and trees, and activity in the streets, but my inner world was always more full of activity than that outside world. I had the solitude to listen more to the clamoring voices within myself with all their contradictory claims. My own hunger for comfort also made stronger the voices of the world's helpless and dependent. They were inside me too.

Ambivalent feelings began to subside. My fear about so large an undertaking as Sarah's Circle lost its dominant place. I knew that, given the chance, I would try to build a community of caring for a segment of the elderly poor in the city.

Praise had helped me discover a sanctuary in myself. I knelt there long enough to know what I was to do. If ever so faintly, I answered, "I'm coming. I'm coming . . ."

25

Witnesses to Praise

Thou that hast given so much to me,
Give one thing more—a grateful heart;
Not thankful when it pleaseth me,
As if Thy blessings had spare days;
But such a heart, whose pulse may be
Thy praise.

George Herbert, Our Prayer

The roar of the world is in my ears.
    Thank God for the roar of the world!
Thank God for the mighty tide of fears
    Against me always hurled!

Thank God for the bitter and ceaseless strife,
    And the sting of His chastening rod!
Thank God for the stress and the pain of life,
    And Oh, thank God for God!

Joyce Kilmer, Thanksgiving

Lord, for the erring thought
Not unto evil wrought:
Lord, for the wicked will
Betrayed and baffled still:
For the heart from itself kept,
Our thanksgiving accept.
For ignorant hopes that were
Broken to our blind prayer:

For pain, death, sorrow sent
Unto our chastisement:
For all loss of seeming good,
Quicken our gratitude.

> William Dean Howells,
> *The Undiscovered Country*

In the morning,
in the night,
in the darkness
and the light
in life's sorrow
and life's joy—
Praise Him.

> Alma Newitt, *Song of the Day*

Oh, Lord of the Universe
I will sing Thee a song.
Where canst Thou be found,
and where canst Thou not be found?
Where I pass—there art Thou.
Where I remain—there, too, Thou art.
Thou, Thou, and only Thou.

Doth it go well—'tis thanks to Thee.
Doth it go ill—ah, 'tis also thanks to Thee.

Thou art, Thou hast been, and Thou wilt be.
Thou didst reign, Thou reignest, and Thou wilt reign.

Thine is Heaven, Thine is Earth.
Thou fillest the high regions,
And Thou fillest the low regions.
Wheresoever I turn, Thou, oh Thou, art there.

> Leon Stein, *Hassidic Music*

Praise is the song
of the spirit
that reaches
a crescendo of joy
in deepest sorrow.

Alma Newitt, *Song of the Day*

In the deserts of the heart
Let the healing fountains start,
In the prison of his days
Teach the free man how to praise.

W. H. Auden, *In Memory of W. B. Yeats*

If anyone could tell you the shortest, surest way to all happiness
and perfection, he must tell you to make it a rule to yourself to
thank and praise God for everything that happens to you. For it
is certain that whatever seeming calamity happens to you, if you
thank and praise God for it, you turn it into a blessing.

William Law

I thank God for my handicaps, for through them I have found
myself, my work and my God.

Helen Keller

The evil which we see everywhere in the world in the form of
affliction and crime is a sign of the distance between us and
God. But this distance is love and therefore it should be loved.
This does not mean loving evil, but loving God through the evil.
When a child in his play breaks something valuable, his mother
does not love the breakage. But if later on her son goes far away
or dies she thinks of the incident with infinite tenderness because she now sees it only as one of the signs of her child's
existence. It is in this way that we ought to love God through
everything good and everything evil, without distinction. If we

love only through what is good, then it is not God we are loving but something earthly to which we give that name. We must not try to reduce evil to good by seeking compensations or justifications for evil. We must love God through the evil that occurs, solely because everything that actually occurs is real and behind all reality stands God. Some realities are more or less transparent; others are completely opaque; but God is behind all of them, without distinction. It is for us simply to keep our eyes turned towards the point where he is, whether we can see him or not. If there were no transparent realities we should have no idea of God. But if all realities were transparent it would not be God but simply the sensation of light that we would be loving. It is when we do not see God, it is when his reality is not sensibly perceptible to any part of our soul, that we have to become really detached from the self in order to love him. That is what it is to love God.

Simone Weil, *Gateway to God*, p. 81.

. . . and for all things give thanks to God, because this is what God expects you to do in Christ Jesus.

1 Thessalonians 5:18

. . . but be filled with the Spirit, addressing one another in psalms and hymns and spiritual songs, singing and making melody to the Lord with all your heart, always and for everything giving thanks in the name of our Lord Jesus Christ to God the Father.

Ephesians 5:18–20, RSV

We know that by turning everything to their good God cooperates with all those who love him, with all those that he has called according to his purpose.

Romans 8:28

To think that one small heart can experience so much, oh God, so much suffering and so much love. I am so grateful to You, God, for having chosen my heart, in these times, to experience all the things it has experienced.

Etty Hillesum

Tell us, Poet, what do you do?
  I praise. But the deadly and the monstrous things, how
    can you bear them?
  I praise. But what is nameless, what is anonymous, how
    can you call upon it?
  I praise. What right have you to be true in every disguise,
    behind every mask?
  I praise. How is it that the calm and the violent things
    like star and storm know you for their own?
Because I praise.

Rainer Maria Rilke

26

On Inner Unity

Response to vision seems to be surrender to the destiny written deep in one's own being. When that surrender is made—"let what you have said be done to me" (Luke 1:38)—one is connected not only to the core of one's own life, but to the pulsating, energizing heart of God at the center of the universe and at the center of every life.

For years I talked in one way or another about Sarah's Circle, but my words quickened nothing in those who heard them. My divided self kept me from speaking with urgency or clarity. My words could not reach that place in others where call is heard. As the conflicts in me were lessened, that began to change.

When I spoke about Sarah's Circle a person here and there listened, and I took note. I was still not ready to issue a call. I did not feel strong enough in myself. Moses had Aaron; Paul had Barnabas. The very name Barnabas means son of encouragement and consolation. Jesus had sent them out by twos so that they might give encouragement and consolation to each other in times of stress. The person who would share and bear equally the burden of the vision of Sarah's Circle had not come. When Sheila Carruth finally appeared I knew her in an instant. When I told her about Sarah's Circle her ready response was, "I want to build such an institution." "I know others," I said, "who will want to build it with us. I will call them." The calling of Sarah's Circle together was not unlike the calling of the twelve. I knew who the members of this group were, where to find them, and what to say. They were quite ready to put aside their ordinary nets and take up this new work.

I might have been amazed at my own power, except that power is not so exceptional as we think. It is always given to those who are committed. It is our divided selves that keep us ineffective and sometimes paralyzed. The temptation story illustrates the terrible division Jesus felt in himself and his hard-achieved surrender to the destiny stamped upon his being. With the work of unity accomplished in himself he moved out in the power of the Spirit to issue the command that every creator of a new order must issue, "Come, follow me." The twelve gathered around Jesus have then the task of resolving the conflicts within themselves so that they can be sent out to be initiating centers of the New Society.

The unity in myself is not complete. Each day I struggle with conflicting claims. I yearn for oneness in myself—for that pure concentration of being that I see in the spiritual genius and of which our age is in such grievous need.

On Fear

Gordon preached a sermon today on fear. He said:

"When I reflect deeply on my life and what I really want, it is not to be afraid. When I am afraid, I am miserable. I play it safe. I restrict myself. I hide the talent of me in the ground. I am not deeply alive—the depths of me are not being expressed. When I am afraid a tiny part of me holds captive most of me which rebels against the tyranny of the minority. When I am afraid I am a house divided against itself. So more than anything else I want to be delivered from fear, for fear is alien to my own best interest or, to put it positively, I want to give myself generously, magnanimously, freely—out of love. I want to be able to take risks—to express myself, to welcome and embrace the future. I want to see what it is to be most deeply me. I want union with all of life and existence. I want to know and sense a oneness with others—with all humankind. I want to know warmth and closeness, to give acceptance and understanding and support. I want to sacrifice myself freely, for this is when I am most alive, most me. I sense that the art of loving, the art of risk taking, is my thing."

In *True Wilderness*, H. A. Williams wrote, ". . . If you want to discover the difference which Jesus made to mankind, and go to the New Testament to find out, the answer given is the casting out of people's lives of fear. Fear, in the New Testament, is considered to be the root of all evil. It is fear which makes men selfish, it is fear which makes them hate, it is fear which makes them blind, it is fear which makes them mad. Fear casts out love, as love casts out fear. Which of the two therefore am I going to choose?"[47]

I turn to these two statements when I feel afraid. They give me courage and aid in the ordering of my own household. We need all the help we can get in battling fear. It is the underlying negative emotion in all and each of us.

My fears keep me from being the self I was intended to be, and from doing the work that is mine to do. Poet Denise Levertov completes the thought:

> I know there is so much of me
> wasted,
> so much we could have been or done
> that we held ourselves back from,
> out of fear,
> or out of the dream we had but one thing to be or do,
> or out of the faith a life is richer lived among paths
>   not taken.[48]

2 8

On Being Satisfied

Today I heard a tape of a class that Thomas Merton taught on the mystical life. What stood out for me was a little story he told from Sufi literature:

> It is related in the traditions that Moses said . . . "Oh God, show me an action wherein if I did it thou wouldst be satisfied." God answered, "Thou canst not do that, Oh Moses." Then Moses fell prostrate worshiping God and supplicating him, and God made a revelation to him and said, "Oh Moses, my satisfaction with thee consists in thy being satisfied with me."

Merton told his class of monks, "I think that is an extremely important principle of the spiritual life—'My satisfaction with thee consists in thy being satisfied with me.' I would say that if a person latched on to that and really absorbed it and really lived it, he would have it made."[49]

Because it seemed to hold so much possibility, I have meditated on this bit of philosophy as one would meditate on a koan. It helps me to relax into my own being and to let what is there unfold. It takes away the motivation of doing something for approval because that approval is already given. It speaks to me of being content with myself, which is easier because the story makes self-acceptance synonymous with acceptance of God. I had never thought before that being critical of myself was being critical of God who made me and even now pronounces me "satisfactory as is." If God is the creator it is not appropriate to rebel against one of his creations, even if that creation is myself. That would be expressing dissatisfaction with God. This does not mean relinquishing my goals for growth, but rejoicing in what is while I reach for what can be. I can give praise for myself as faulted as I am, and then take the next step. In this response God is not only the One who goes before me, but is *God with me*. The journey then is important—not where I will be tomorrow and what I will do when I arrive at my destination.

In giving praise for ourselves we become more aware of how many strains of self-hatred weave through our self-love. We are misguided when we worry about the people who think too well of themselves. Our wars with each other are grounded in self-hatred, not self-love.

Meister Eckhart said that when he was born all creation stood up and said, "God is!" I know that for truth, but I cannot imagine writing those words about myself. That I flowed out from God is not deep enough in my unconscious. Most of us have not known that we celebrate God in the world when we celebrate ourselves. If only there were someone to lean over every crib and to whisper into every new pair of ears, "God is!" We can also do that for each other as adults. We have the power to confirm one another, if we choose. Only one thing is necessary if we are to exercise that power, and that is to become contemplatives. In an article on "Contemplation as Total Awareness," Msgr. William Shannon wrote:

> We have to become *aware* of our relationships with other people: our families, our friends, the people we work with. We have to see the good in these relationships. For the good is what is there. The "bad" in a relationship is what is not there. When we concentrate on what is not there, we fail to experience the good that is there. The same applies to our work. There may be certain elements we want to be there, but actually they are not. Again, if our whole attention is focused on what is not there, we miss the experience of the reality that is there.[50]

When we become reconciled to ourselves we see the good that is there; we cease to make an idol of perfection and become reconciled to God, and reconciled to each other. In Sarah's Circle Fern Edwards was talking very passionately about this. She was citing the Good News translation of 2 Corinthians 5:18 which reads, "All this is done by God, who through Christ changed us from enemies into his friends and gave us the task of making others his friends also." She said that her life was turned around when the meaning of that Scripture broke for her. She knew that although she might have enemies, she did not have the option of being an enemy. Moreover she had the task of changing every enemy into a friend. This is the way we make others into friends of Christ. The man or woman in God will be a person of unconditional love.

On Monday night I was reviewing with Jimilu Mason these three thoughts:

1. Being satisfied with God
2. Seeing the good in every one
3. Choosing not to be the enemy

We talked about how the practice of the above might apply to people in public office whose policies cause suffering among the poor. We decided we would have to give up talking about these officials as enemies and begin perceiving them as friends with whom we were in serious disagreement. I told Jimilu that, as a counselor, the more I come to understand a person the more I come to love that person. She then told me how she had hated Richard Nixon when she began working on a bust of him. "I loathed the man," she said, "when I began that piece. When it was finished, I liked him."

The artist is always the contemplative—the one who sees what is there. The uninhibited three-year-old, stopping with enthralled gaze to watch an insect, or some activity in the street, is also a contemplative. If we could recover that lost capacity to look, which we all once had, we might be able to penetrate to the heart of matters.

Juliana of Norwich, holding "a little thing, the size of a hazelnut," in the palm of her hand, wrote, "In this little thing, I saw three properties. The first is that God made it. The second is that God loves it. The third is that God keeps it."[51] I wonder if that understanding is not essential for any meaningful survival. Our God has made, loves, and keeps us all.

29

Call Unfolding

Members of Sarah's Circle met for the second time with the tenants who live in the building that Jubilee Housing has bought and made available for the elderly. It was easier to think about relocating these tenants in other Jubilee buildings before we had seen their faces. Since our meeting with them we have abandoned that idea altogether. We had dreamed our dream for an empty building and this one is more than half full of tenants who believe that their survival depends on their staying. Friends and advisers have pointed out our legal rights, but somehow these rights do not seem to be important, perhaps because Christianity is both simpler and more complex than the law or than any abstract understanding of the good, based as it is upon a God-man who complicated things by the simple act of breaking bread with strangers and outcasts.

For some of the tenants the building has been home for as long as eighteen years, and these past years have been a nightmare. On the coldest days there was no heat. The plumbing is always in need of repair, and the elevators do not work at all. One woman who suffers with arthritis and wears a leg brace climbs three flights of stairs to her apartment. A leaking roof has made the top floor uninhabitable. Still the people who are left in the building do not want to be uprooted. They do not believe that there is a better place to go. Landlords have lied to them for years and they are not about to trust the new one with the name of Jubilee. One owner after the other has bought the building for tax purposes, milked it of everything possible, and moved on to new fields of plunder. It is a familiar tale in the cities.

The landlords in their turn have had their own troubles. Rents have been frozen too long at prices far too low to allow for proper maintenance. Working through the courts the last owner finally succeeded in doubling the rents for most of the apartments. Though the new rents were still far below the average in the city, the tenants were stunned and angry. In time they secured the free services of student lawyers from Antioch Law School and instituted their own court cases. Jubilee inherited this situation when the building passed into their hands. In the midst of all this anger and confusion Jubilee tried to tell its story, which sounded far-fetched, complicated as it was by being strangely related to the exodus of the Hebrews from oppression in the land of Egypt.

Jubilee takes its name from the fiftieth year which, according to the Book of Leviticus, was to be a year-long celebration of freedom. In this fiftieth year all debts were to be forgiven. In the meantime the biblical people intended to break the cycle of poverty by giving to the poor and the weak the tools necessary to lift themselves out of dependency. The plan was for a society based on justice and compassion. Fifty years seemed a realistic time-frame for such a radical restructuring of the social order. In awkward ways the people of Jubilee and Sarah's Circle claim that their vision is the same, but the people sitting around in a tenement lobby in the richest capital in the world do not believe it, and why should they believe it? Where in the long history of Israel, the New Testament church, or the modern church is it recorded that the Jubilee year ever took place? In the present situation rumors abound and wild tales flourish. Even those who think there might be something to Jubilee's story harbor the suspicion that there may be yet a new form of bondage. In one way or another the tenants say that it is their understanding that they will have to attend the Jubilee Church and subscribe to its beliefs. Although that may seem an absurd idea, the Christian Church does have a long history of giving mission beds and meals to those who come in time for the vesper service and stay for morning worship.

There are other misunderstandings. "You talk about our working together to make possible this dream of a new society. What does that mean? Does it mean collecting everyone's garbage, or scrubbing down the steps each day? I'm willing to do my share, but some things I am not willing to do." The work we had intended was the work of creation. In the tenants' experience that work meant the kind that wracks the bones and leaves life and spirit wasted.

The Antioch lawyers appointed to represent the tenants are half convinced that Jubilee really is on the side of their clients and means what it says. They point out to the tenants that this is the first time an owner has ever sat down with them and talked about what might go into a new contract and asked for their help in shaping a program. "You have to admit that this is different." There is silence. No one is willing to agree so early in the dialogue. Sitting in the midst of the tenants, I am stabbed by my own secret doubts. We in Sarah's Circle sometimes have a hard time communicating with one another, saying what we mean and being understood, bearing the burden of each other's darkness. How much more difficult communication will be between two such diverse groups, one predominantly white, the other, black. Moreover, no matter how earnest our words, the tenants fear we are the enemy.

One of their leaders wants to know more about Sarah's Circle. We tell them what we know and, in the telling, grow more aware that we are describing our mission, not theirs.

"We have nothing against the elderly," a spokesman for the tenants says, "but what about us? What is going to happen to us?" "How do we fit in?" asks another. A more hostile person says, "Why did you have to pick this building? Why don't you just go away and leave us alone?"

We explain that the building was on the market, and sooner or later would have gone to a real estate developer able to convert it into high-cost condominiums. "This is happening all around you," we say. "It was going to happen here too." We carefully say that when we planned Sarah's Circle we wanted to bring in children from the neighborhood and have programs that would attract persons of all ages. "This has changed since meeting with you. We want now to build with you an intergenerational community. You can keep on living here. Only the vacant apartments will be made into studio apartments for the elderly." We talk a long time about a community where older persons will grandparent children and where the present tenants in turn can choose to be in relationship with people who are at a vulnerable stage in life and need the security that a caring network will give. We talk about raising money to convert the basement into common rooms and a dining area where older persons can have at least one good meal a day—a place to be used by all the tenants for festive occasions and educational programs.

A tenant interrupts to declare that to be impossible. The basement is the place where the dealers on the street stash their drugs. Another suggests, "It is that way now, but when Sarah's Circle moves in, the drug traffic will move out." Another voice injects, "My nephew was beat up down there." "Stop talking that way," our new defender says. "That can change! Listen to them!"

We have the floor again, and this time I speak. I tell them that I am afraid of promising too much because we have no funds; that our dream for the building is dependent on our raising money from foundations and individuals in the churches who care about what is happening in the cities, and who know that we are better human beings when we care for each other.

Now that the subject of money has been raised the conversation shifts to more immediate needs and focuses on the Jubilee lease, which the tenants have been asked to sign. "It states in this lease," says one man, "that we may not have pets in the building. I have had my dog for twelve years," he says. "My dog is like a person. You don't ask anyone to give up a person."

"Oh, no," the chorus goes up from members of Sarah's Circle. "We want to have pets in the building. Today pets are being introduced into programs for the elderly."

The man scoffs at this middle-class enlightenment. "I have my pet for protection. You may get drugs out of the basement, but you won't get them off the streets. Open that door and there it is."

A young mother says, "I am allergic to cat fur, but I have a cat to keep the mice out of my apartment." Another mother adds, "I had a rat in my apartment last week. It was no mouse! I called five departments in this city including the police and no one would help me get rid of it."

The primary issue, however, is none of these things. The real concern is increased rents and how they will be paid. That subject is finally addressed. The tenants who have come to this meeting seem to be the working poor, though one is a very old man and another says she is living on a Social Security check. Those who work could probably get from welfare as much as they earn from working the whole week, but they have no intention of giving up the dignity of employment. Their terror is that they cannot figure out how they can pay the increased rent. Jubilee and Sarah's Circle must figure how to push those rents back without raising funds to subsidize them—an almost impossible thing to do. Housing for the poor does not capture the imagination of very many.

We all agree that we will meet in three weeks to talk again. In the meantime the operating costs go on and Sarah's Circle and Jubilee are locked in afresh with the poor and their struggle for survival. On the way home I confide to Esther Dorsey that for the first time I am glad Sarah's Circle has no money as yet. If we walked into their building and were able to carry out our plan, the tenants might feel like beneficiaries rather than participants. As it is we must engage them in the planning and fund-raising process. "Maybe we can do that," responds Esther, "but don't expect them to believe that you are not rich. Poor black people think all white people are rich. When you are poor there is no other way to understand what you see and hear."

I remembered the large woman who sat by the door and muttered under her breath loud enough for us all to hear. "None of you lives in a place like this."

30

The Builder Is God

I meditated today on the first chapter of 1 Samuel. What suffering and beauty in the story of Hannah, the mother of Samuel. Yearning for a child and taunted by her rivals because she was barren, Hannah fell into a severe depression. She lost her appetite and could only weep. Her husband, who loved her more than he loved any other human being, tried his best to comfort her. In plaintive words he asked, "Hannah, why are you crying and why are you not eating? Why so sad? Am I not more to you than ten sons?" Distraught, she ran from the dining hall to stand beside the priest Eli while she poured out her heart to God: "Yahweh Sabaoth! If you will take notice of the distress of your servant, and bear me in mind and not forget your servant and give her a man-child, I will give him to Yahweh for the whole of his life . . ."

When the prayer was answered and a son born to Hannah, she knew that he was not hers, but the Lord's. When she had nursed Samuel through his infant years, and made him independent of a mother's close nurturing, she took her small son and went again to see Eli: "As you live, my lord, I am the woman who stood here beside you praying to Yahweh. This is the child I prayed for, and Yahweh granted me what I asked him. Now I make him over to Yahweh for the whole of his life. He is made over to Yahweh."

As with Isaac, Samson, and John the Baptist, Samuel was born to a woman who was aware that she was not going to produce offspring unless God intervened. Their barrenness and their petitions gave all of these women a covenantal relationship with God. They would never cling to their children or claim them as their own. The mother of Jesus had this same understanding of parenthood though she had not suffered in the same way. What would it mean for the nurture of our children, if we believed that they were God's, that he had a purpose for them, and that our task was to instruct them in listening to what that might be, and then to let them go?

In like manner, is not the new creative work stirring in us God's work? I pray to him that we can nurture Sarah's Circle in the womb of our lives, hover over it until it is safely delivered, then dedicate it to God and never seek to possess it. Institutions, like persons, take on a life and an energy of their own. Too often our own ambitions and striving for a place in the scheme of things enter in and keep them from growing according to the ways of God—a work intended for the poor becomes stunted and self-serving.

Let us remember that we are barren now. We have not produced the institution of our vision. If our prayer is granted and it is born of our hard labor, let us pray again for Hannah's strength to place the child of our dreaming in God's hands for the whole of its life, that it may become his word in the universe.

3 1

On Giving

Last night we gave a fund-raising banquet for Sarah's Circle at the headquarters building of The Church of The Saviour, an old Victorian mansion on Massachusetts Avenue. The high-ceilinged rooms with their graceful arches never looked more beautiful. Mary Jo Cook, who has the gift of making rooms light up, had decorated with branches of azalea blossoms. The candles and napkins matched the pink in the flowers. Joan Martin, who is allergic to gas fumes, wore a white mask and cooked on the church gas stove a gourmet meal for seventy-five persons. Sheila Carruth's trays of hors d'oeuvres looked like studies for a gourmet magazine, and all of us were in our dress-up clothes. Altogether it was a shining and lavish event—with no speech too long.

Looking around the room one would not have been impressed with the wealth of the group, but gatherings of this kind have a way of turning into stories of loaves and fishes. When the evening was over, contributions and pledges amounted to $52,000.

The most moving gift was from Beulah Rivers, who, because of childhood polio, must wear a heavy brace on one leg. A tenant on the third floor of the Sarah's Circle building, Beulah suffers from arthritis made even more painful by climbing up and down the stairs. One time when she could not walk at all, children in the building devised an ingenious solution for getting her out into the community. They put a pillow on a blanket, and Beulah on the pillow, and half-carried, half-tugged this beautiful, aching woman down three flights of stairs. They then went back for her wheelchair. The children could not manage to get her up the stairs but there were always men hanging around the alley who could be coaxed into tugging and carrying her back to her apartment. They still help her with her groceries, so that Beulah knows better than most the importance of intergenerational living, and has thrilled to the dream of Sarah's Circle. To support the project she is selling used clothing and other items on a nearby street corner. Her contribution last night was the telling of her story, a check for $180, and a commitment of half of her future profits. The other half is going to the Jubilee Loan Fund.

Today I stopped to visit with Beulah at her sidewalk store. While I was there she sold a woman a pair of almost new shoes for seventy-five cents. Later I asked her why she had sold them for so little. "She is one of my people," said Beulah. "She lives on a $240 welfare check. I know their stories, I know the ones who go home and get beat up, and the ones who need food. When I was a drunk in these streets and fell down, these were the ones who picked me up. These are all my people. They, and everyone else who buys from me, know about Sarah's Circle. Sometimes I'm hoarse when I go home at night from talking about it."

Beulah's apartment is the meeting place of the AA group she founded. Her street stand is also a drop-in counseling center for AA members who know that this wonderfully generous and noble woman is always available to listen and to give encouragement. In one day she counsels effectively as many people as any well-established therapist.

32

On Creativity

Early this morning Beulah was held up. She was hanging clothes on her new garment rack on the pavement outside the Columbia Road Laundromat when four young men approached her. One of them pulled out a knife and held it against her chest. "For a moment," she said, "the fear I felt was real. Then my eyes fell on the Sarah's Circle pamphlets I always keep on the table. Automatically a peace came into me. 'I got but fifteen dollars,' I told him, 'and that ain't mine. That belongs to the Almighty.' The knife disappeared. I don't know when it happened, but it disappeared. I reached for one of the brochures. I wasn't sure that he could read, but that's all right, because sometimes from one street person to another you can draw pictures. Then my eyes lit on Christ House and I said, 'See that building across the street? The same church people are fixing up that building. One day you're going to be able to walk in there and take a shower and have a place where you can lay down. You'll be able to go there without a dime in the world and be treated like a person.' I don't usually speak that calm and peaceful," said Beulah. "I am usually a loud-mouth, but this time I said the right words.

"'But lady,' one of the young men said, 'We need some clothes.'

"'You don't have to pull a knife on me to get clothes,' I told him, 'You're welcome to the clothes.' I saw that he had a hole in his shoe. I picked up a pair of shoes and said, 'Maybe these shoes will fit you?' When I said that he gave the knife to one of the others and the three left—but he stayed around the whole day, helping me out now and then.

"I usually give only half the money I make to Sarah's Circle," she added. "The other half I give to the Jubilee Loan Fund, in case I might need it some time. But today I'm giving it all to Sarah's Circle."

Beulah told us that selling the used clothes makes her feel useful. "I love being in on the start of Sarah's Circle. Today some contractors came to look around the basement and my heart was jumping with excitement. I wake up each day eager for what the next thing will be."

Those of us in Sarah's Circle have that same excitement. Despite our weariness with many meetings, we keep rejoicing that we have the opportunity to create this institution. When we reflect on how wonderful is the feeling of being chosen, and letting ourselves be chosen, it becomes abundantly evident that creativity is everyone's vocation—the only faithful response that we can make to God's call.

Perhaps more significantly than any other writer, Nikolai Berdyaev has influenced my thinking about creativity. He feels it is imperative to bear in mind that human creativeness is not a claim or a right on the part of men and women, but God's claim on, and call to each one of us. "God awaits man's creative act, which is the response to the creative act of God."

In many of his books Berdyaev stresses God's need of men and women, a teaching not mentioned in traditional, orthodox Christianity. This omission strips revelation of its central message, and confirms humankind in a false dependent state rather than awakening men and women to an awareness of themselves as persons with the power and responsibility of transfiguring themselves and transfiguring the earth. Berdyaev states:

> The idea of God is the greatest human idea, and the idea of man is the greatest divine idea. Man awaits the birth of God in himself, and God awaits the birth of man in himself. It is at this level that the question of creativity arises, and it is from this point of view that it should be approached. The notion that God has need of man and of man's response to him is admittedly an extraordinarily daring notion; yet in its absence the Christian revelation of God-manhood loses all meaning. The drama of

God and his Other One, Man, is present and operative in the very depth of divine life.[52]

For Berdyaev creation is a vocation that demands heroism and suffering, but it also takes us into an eternally green world. Creativity is always prophetic, always directed toward the future, reaching out to the infinite. While it belongs to the eternal, creative power seeks to manifest itself in a world which is situated in evil. True creativeness is a fight against evil, greed, boredom, and emptiness. "The ethics of creativeness," wrote Berdyaev, "is an ethics of struggle and contemplation."

> It is an ethics of both ascent and of descent. The human soul rises upwards, ascends to God, wins for itself the gifts of the Holy Spirit and strives for aristocratism. But it also descends into the sinful world, shares the fate of the world and of other men, strives to help its brothers and gives them the spiritual energy acquired in the upward movement of the soul.[53]

Creative power is hidden away in everyone's being. The experience of it is possible for me and for Beulah, for the man with the knife, the drug dealers on the corner, and for everyone who will come to live in Sarah's Circle. We each can become a creator because we have within us the image of the great Creator. God in Christ calls us to the work of completing our lives and completing the earth, of doing something that has never been done before. Though we may have only a tiny spark or smoldering wick within us, our task is to fan it into fire. This is the gospel that Sarah's Circle wants to proclaim—the human-divine vocation to be creators. We want to mount that summit of daring, which Berdyaev says is reached in the awareness that on men and women depends not human life alone, but divine life as well. These days I know this best as I walk through the rotting rooms of the Sarah's Circle building, and listen to contractors talk about a roof that needs replacing, a heating system that will last only a few more months, and an elevator that may never work again. The powerlessness of God without us is disconcertingly evident. The other half of this truth is equally apparent. I am burningly aware of our need of him. Without an infusion of his spirit into the lives of those who carry the vision of Sarah's Circle, beauty, justice, forgiveness, liberating love, mercy, compassion—these qualities which are the essence of Christianity—will not abound in those rooms and halls.

33

More on Money

If Sarah's Circle is to have an incarnational life we must raise over a million dollars this year. This means that everyone in Sarah's Circle must become a fund-raiser. The idea is startling to all of us and repelling to some. Most of us would rather give than ask for money, and now we find ourselves the organizers and architects of what will have to be a gigantic fund-raising program. How else does one raise a million dollars! More than this we are not sure that we will ever see an end to it. Even when our building is renovated, the elderly poor who come to live there may need to have their rents subsidized. It is no small horror to think we might be fund-raisers for the rest of our lives when we had it in mind to be poets, prophets, and protectors of the common good. The work before us seems overwhelming enough without our having to take on a task for which we have no inclination or experience, and perhaps no capability.

Our distress is so great that we are feeling a bit hostile as though we have been weighted with too large a burden. We shared our concern today with Dick Uhle who agreed that raising money is difficult and that it is a sobering experience to think about asking people for large amounts of money. He went on to say, however, that it is sheer fantasy to think that anyone is likely to come in and do it for us. He cheered us a little by emphasizing the fact that across this country were many persons who would want to be a part of the spiritual adventure that Sarah's Circle is, and that our work was simply to find them. "What you offer," he said, "is a relationship with yourselves and a relationship with the poor of this country. You are not raising money—you are building a community." His emphasis on community and the importance of prayer helped to restore our spirits.

Being more calm in myself, I am able to reflect that all of our missions have had to raise their own money, and this has been immensely good for us. It has helped us to purge the dross from our thinking and clarify our own commitment. When competing for funds from corporations and foundations, one must accept the disciplines of rigorous prayer, thought, and study. Missions, like people, must go through a purification process if they are to live, and I doubt that that ever happens unless those with visions are willing or forced to deal with money. For any marriage between heaven and earth, contemplatives also need to grapple day in and day out with economics.

34

Money Again

Last night Gordon Cosby talked to Sarah's Circle about fund-raising. He began by saying that he had met with a lot of groups discussing fund-raising, and that he finds without exception that their own attitude toward money is their greatest obstacle to raising it. He said, "People working for the poor tend to treat money as the enemy. They resent having to raise it. The implication often is 'We are laying down our lives for the poor—others ought to provide the money.' We are all stuck in the materialism of our age. Very few people are free about money.

Deal with your own ambivalences concerning it. Let your response to mission be wholistic—include your money as well as your time."

Gordon's second point was that fund-raising is a means of education. "In interpreting the dream, you are helping people to redefine the way they relate to the poor and the old, as well as to redefine the way they relate to their own aging. Money is an exciting dimension of the mission and makes possible hundreds of wonderful conversations. Because your mission needs money you will be motivated to get out there and to talk to people about a whole new realm—things about which you would not speak in the ordinary course of events. Be glad you are not starting out with money. When you have it you attract people who are looking for work and who want to make a career out of serving the poor. They see the project as a way of breaking into the political arena. When you have money people want jobs with you for the salaries they will receive and the careers they will further. When you have no money there is no mistaking who is called."

Thirdly, Gordon reminded us to ground our efforts in prayer. "Really believe that God has called you. The resources will come through your efforts, but they are not rooted in your efforts. The power to create the new comes only through God. You must make solitude a part of your days, and let your action flow out of your contemplation and God's care for the poor. This does not mean shifting onto God what does not belong to him. Too much sickness goes under the name of trusting in God. Be responsible co-creators."

Finally Gordon said, "The money you raise will be in direct proportion to the number of people you ask. Never make your asking a demand, or put your dream in such a way that people will have to reject you if they do not support your dream. We have no right to assume that others should support our vision. State your vision as compellingly as you can state it; then leave others free to make whatever response is right for them to make."

35

God's Dependence

Gordon's words gave us fresh energy. It was a long time, however, before they took deep root in me. I found hints of transformation in myself on the day that Sheila Carruth and I went scavenging for refrigerators and stoves.

Carpenters and other workmen are busy renovating half of the top floor of Sarah's Circle—turning two wings into seven attractive efficiencies and a large sitting room. They will begin work on the other two wings of that floor when additional funds become available. Sheila and I, wanting the kitchens to have new stoves and refrigerators, priced them at Sears only to find their cost beyond our means. We decided that before settling for shabby second-hand equipment, we would visit plumbing and kitchen firms in the area. We spent the day going from retailer to retailer. In each place we were referred to the proper person in the organization and shared our hope that those who came to live in Sarah's Circle might have a shining kitchen, maybe a bathroom, too. We were bold to ask whether the firm ever did any "in-house" giving, or had good second-hand appliances they might want to contribute or sell. One man promised to let us know about reduced, dented items; a woman said that she was quite hopeful that she could find us several used refrigerators in good condition. No one actually gave us anything, but everyone seemed glad to know about Sarah's Circle. As the day moved on we took more joy in telling our story.

I never think of that day without remembering the monks I had seen on the streets of Bangkok when I visited there. Each morning they were on the sidewalks of the city. People walking by would slip money or food into the small bowls they carried. I was perplexed and saddened by their begging. I did not comprehend how they could allow themselves to be dependent on the grace and mercy of others for their very existence. Now I begin to understand. For a few hours I had been a beggar of sorts on the streets of my own city. I had done my alms' rounds for those whose future is also utterly dependent on the grace and mercy of others. This, however, is quite different from having to beg on behalf of one's self. I am afraid to pray for that much humility. I have too much dread of being dependent— unable to care for my own needs. I do what I can to protect myself against such a possibility. My anxious wishes make me a strong advocate of IRA accounts, and retirement plans, but my heart no longer rests easily with the ways I secure my future. In contemplating the Christmas child this year I am more aware that God's existence in this world is dependent on grace and mercy in me, as well as in monks and governments.

Madeleine L'Engle writes:

> This is the irrational season
> when love blooms bright and wild.
> Had Mary been filled with reason
> There'd have been no room for the child.[54]

My prayer:

> Lord Jesus, come again
> Thy spirit to impart.
> Make as an empty inn
> My lone and fearful heart.

36

The Thinking Heart

Ever since the book, *An Interrupted Life: The Diaries of Etty Hillesum, 1941-1943*, was put into my hands, it has been kept close by my side so that I can pick it up and meditate on an underlined passage or read a selected paragraph to a friend. Now nothing will do except for me to go back and reread it. Although I am trying to read more slowly this time, it is difficult for I am hungry for the words in this book. I know that when I have come to the end I will have to go back and begin all over again. What is there in these pages that breathes life into me, bestows spirit, and evokes energy? I ponder that question.

Etty was Jewish, living in German-occupied Amsterdam when she began writing in the first of what would be eight exercise books. She was twenty-seven years of age, a fact, which having read her diary, I find astounding. Though I have been committed to fighting the stereotyping of the old, I have had to confront reverse ageist notions in myself. Etty Hillesum helps me with that task. I did not think that anyone of her years could be so wise. Brilliant, gifted, stimulating—yes, but wise? No. There is heart knowledge that the young do not have simply because they have not lived long enough, or so I thought.

Perhaps it was the hard and cruel times that she endured that quickly brought depth to Etty's young life. One finds the same precociousness in the girl Anne Frank who, hidden away in a house not far from where Etty lived, was writing her diary at about the same time. When large inner and outer events are compressed into a short time span they must combine to mature the heart in a way that ordinarily would not be possible; or perhaps, as Etty thought, one can be born with a thousand-year-old soul. In any case, I find in Etty Hillesum not only a guide and teacher, but a life that I want to touch again and again. I want my soul to know her soul.

For me Christ's central message has always been that we can have as intimate a relationship with God as the one he knew. He is the firstborn, the elder brother, and we are sisters and brothers, heirs with him to an utterly new world. Etty Hillesum makes that message vibrate once more in my own being. In her the fullness of God was pleased to dwell, and I am alive with that possibility for myself, for the street people, the man at the cash register who rings up the charge for my coffee and toast each morning, Miss Bessie who is sixty and wants to learn to read, and for everyone else who crosses my path. I want to whisper in their ears the news of their divinity, though it is probably quite sufficient that I keep fresh that awareness in my own heart.

In her first entry, March 9, 1941, Etty Hillesum wrote:

> . . . I seem to be a match for most of life's problems, and yet deep down something like a tightly wound ball of twine binds me relentlessly and at times I am nothing more or less than a miserable, frightened creature, despite the clarity with which I can express myself.[55]

One of her last diary entries was written on August 18, 1943, not long before she was put on a cattle train bound for Auschwitz:

> You have made me so rich, oh God, please let me share out Your beauty with open hands. My life has become an uninterrupted dialogue with You, oh God, one great dialogue. Sometimes when I stand in some corner of the camp, my feet planted on Your earth, my eyes raised towards Your Heaven, tears sometimes run down my face, tears of deep emotion and gratitude. At night, too, when I lie in my bed and rest in You, oh God, tears of gratitude run down my face, and that is my prayer . . .[56]

I find Etty teaching me to pray and to keep a journal though these are subjects I have taught and written about. Not that her book tells us how to do anything. Its power lies in the fact that it admits us into the presence of a person writing in a journal, a person praying, a person in a walk with God. What we find ourselves witnessing is the transformation of a human life. The experience for me is like being on the Mount of Transfiguration. I begin to understand the luminous nature of that event.

Etty Hillesum was a well-educated and an extraordinarily gifted young woman. She was also very modern and secular when she began her journal. Her exercise books give expression to an intense emotional life. One feels awe at her openness to what is happening in her and what appears to be her easy access to a wide range of feelings. I am reminded of my own unconscious sleeping state at her age and how unable I was to make order of the turmoil in myself. She used her journal to record the world inside her, to sort through her feelings and give them shelter. She wrote not only to gain clarity, but to find and listen to her own inner voice, and to make that voice her guide. "When I pray," she wrote, "I hold a silly, naïve or deadly serious dialogue with what is deepest inside me, which for convenience sake I call God." Through the pages of the book one watches her relationship with God deepen and grow until God is the ground of being—the arms in which she is safe, and also the transcendent God whose immanence is in everything she sees and hears.

Because Etty strove for wholeness, she sought and found a counselor. He was Julius Spier, a fifty-four-year-old Jewish emigrant from Berlin, who had had analysis training with Carl Jung. With Jung's encouragement Spier himself became a therapist and guide. He was a powerful source of energy for Etty and scores of people, mostly young, whom he taught and counseled in his exile. After a few sessions with him Etty became his secretary, then a friend and close companion in his work. Under his tutelage she felt her life growing and expanding, though one guesses that that would inevitably have happened for her in one way or another.

Etty fell in love with her mentor. She was able to recognize and accept Spier's frailties which never hindered her growing love and admiration. She knew very early, however, that she had to become a separate person—"get him out of her system without running away." In the company of S., as she called him, Etty grew in self-reliance and independence, and finally broke free to stand on her own feet with a love that reached out to embrace all of life. She writes, "The foolish and passionate desire to love myself in him has long ago vanished, has grown 'sensible.' All I have left of that feeling is the will to 'yield' myself up to God, or to a poem."

A still needed note in women's literature is Etty's naturalness in conveying and exploring her own sexuality. At home in her body, she was unafraid of the sensual in herself, a fact which will help readers to open to this dimension in themselves. It is, however, a matter of great concern to me that allusions to her sexuality in the early sections of her book may make the book forbidden reading in large segments of the church. That would be a great and grievous loss.

As concisely as any modern feminist, Etty examined the role of women and took a penetrating look at the man-woman relationship in a few short paragraphs:

> It's not at all simple, the role of women. Sometimes, when I pass a woman in the street, a beautiful, well-groomed, wholly feminine, albeit dull woman, I completely lose my poise. Then I feel that my intellect, my struggle, my suffering, are oppressive, ugly, unwomanly; then I, too, want to be beautiful and dull, a desirable plaything for a man. It's typical that I always do end up wanting to be desired by a man, the ultimate confirmation of our worth and womanhood, but in fact it is only a primitive instinct. Feelings of friendship, respect and love for us as human beings, these are all very well, but don't we ultimately want men to desire us as women? It is almost too difficult for me to write down all I feel; the subject is infinitely complex, but it is altogether too important not to be discussed.
>
> Perhaps the true, the essential emancipation of women still has to come. We are not yet full human beings; we are the "weaker sex." We are still tied down and enmeshed in centuries-old

traditions. We still have to be born as human beings, that is the great task that lies before us.[57]

Writers such as Rilke, Dostoevsky, Jung, and the apostles seem to be the ones who formed and nourished Etty's life. These are the ones that she kept close by her side. They were the ones in her rucksack when she went to Westerbork, and the ones she so fervently wanted to keep with her when her turn came to leave the camp for Auschwitz. She was especially drawn to the Gospel of St. Matthew. She mentioned Jesus by name only once, but his were the words she cited. From her pen, in the circumstances under which she wrote, those words, so familiar to Christians, have a new transforming power. She especially noted Matthew 6:34: "Take therefore no thought for the morrow: for the morrow shall take thought for the things of itself." Surrounded by human misery, aware of the destruction of her people, and with her own destruction almost certain, she prayed, "I shall promise You one thing, God, just one very small thing: I shall never burden my today with cares about my tomorrow."[58] I, who have always been a worrier and who, contrary to Gospel teachings, have leaped ahead to anticipate tomorrow's difficulties, bow my head often now and promise God that I will not burden my today with worries about tomorrow.

The circumstances in which I pray have the appearance of being so much less menacing than those in which Etty shared her prayer that the simple utterance of her words restores my perspective. At other times I think that I see signs of approaching destruction—the unravelling of our civilization. So much in the climate of our cities and nation seems ominous.

Etty Hillesum's journal is to the very end concerned more with inner events than outer events. She notes increasing numbers of arrests, the murder of a professor, another's suicide, more demand visits to the headquarters of the gestapo, new restrictions on places Jews may walk and eat, and finally the requirement to wear the yellow star of David. Although these events are entered in Etty's journal, in the first part they do not seem to take enough of her attention. One begins to wonder whether she was as well-informed as she might have been of the seriousness of her situation, and then, in a sentence or two, she lets her reader know how fully aware she was:

> I am sometimes so distracted by all the appalling happenings around me that it's far from easy to find the way back to myself. And yet that's what I must do. I mustn't let myself be ground down by the misery outside.

Most poignant for me are those lines in which now and then she expresses the ardent wish that she might endure to chronicle the history of the days in which she is living.

> And if we should survive unhurt in body and soul, but above all in soul, without bitterness and without hatred, then we shall have a right to a say after the war. Maybe I am an ambitious woman: I would like to have just a tiny little bit of a say.[59]

These lines give me such pain that I can only guess that my own heart does not fully believe that Etty knows her wish has been granted.

When the round-up of Jews began for internment in Westerbork camp, the place from which a transport train left weekly for Auschwitz, Etty's friends urged her to go into hiding. She refused. Although there were those who accused her of indifference and passivity, hers was a different way. She wanted to share the common fate of her people and to share with them her understanding of an imperishable world. Besides, it did not matter very much to her whether she was inside a camp or outside. She had become a free person. Barbed wire fences could not take that freedom away. When Christ makes you free, you are free indeed.

Etty voluntarily went to Westerbork, but eventually the identity card that permitted her to make trips back to Amsterdam was taken away and she became an official camp inmate. In Westerbork her life continued as one "great dialogue" with God.

Truly, my life is one long hearkening unto my self and unto
others, unto God. And if I say that I hearken, it is really God
who hearkens inside me. The most essential and the deepest in
me hearkening unto the most essential and deepest in the other.
God to God.[60]

"God to God," Etty writes. She had received as had Meister
Eckhart, William Blake, Thomas Merton, and every other mystic before her the message of her divinity.

Caution against hatred is one of the themes that runs through
Etty's diaries. She counseled her friends against bitterness, ad-
vising them to turn inward and destroy in themselves what they
thought should be destroyed in others.

Against every new outrage and every fresh horror we shall put
up one more piece of love and goodness, drawing strength from
within ourselves.[61]

Suffering was another important theme for Etty. Early she
noted that S. healed people by teaching them how to suffer and
to accept. She knew that we suffer most through our fears of
suffering, and that "real suffering is always fruitful and can turn
life into a precious thing . . ." Her words might sound idealis-
tic and thus lack power, were she not writing them against a
backdrop of unspeakable suffering and cruelty. She was ministering to starved, exhausted people, to terror-stricken people,
to crying and dying babies and their desperate and doomed
parents. Her own health was poor. Her parents were in the
same camp and, while Etty knew she could bear her own suffering, she was uncertain of being able to watch what her
parents would have to endure. At the heart of that terrible
misery—in hell itself—trying to accommodate herself to the
harder days that loomed on the horizon, she writes the last
words in her diary: "We should be willing to act as a balm for all
wounds."

Etty left her diaries in the hands of a friend, asking her to
give them to Klaas Smelik and his daughter when the war was

over. Klaas was a writer and the one person she knew who might have a contact with a publisher. In the years following the war many publishers did see the diaries but, comprising over four-hundred pages of almost illegible handwriting, they probably posed too formidable a task. In any case, no publisher seems to have recognized their significance, or read far enough to know that he was holding in his hands what to me is the most spiritually significant document of our age. In 1980 the exercise books were given to J. G. Gaarlandt, a Holland publisher. He was immediately captured by the first sentences, and the long work of deciphering Etty's handwriting began. My hope is that one day soon we will have her diaries in their entirety.

The book includes Etty's letters from Westerbork, bearing witness to the last days of the history she lived and to the fairer world she saw so vividly:

> . . . When a spider spins its web, does it not cast the main threads ahead of itself, and then follow along them from behind? The main path of my life stretches like a long journey before me and already reaches into another world. It is just as if everything that happens here and that is still to happen were somehow discounted inside me, as if I had been through it already, and was now helping to build a new and different society.[62]

Etty's life was not taken from her. She laid it down of her own free accord. More than anything hers is the story of a journey into freedom.

Besides the diaries and letters, Etty left one more piece of writing. Out of the windows of the train that carried her to Auschwitz where she died on November 30, 1943, she flung a postcard which was later picked up by a farmer. On it she had scribbled her last message to us, "We have left the camp singing."

37

A Mature Spirituality

Like every story of creation the story of Sarah's Circle is one of agony and ecstasy, of pain and hope. I wonder if the ingredients of creativity are ever different, since we hold our divinity in earthenware vessels.

Some days I have wanted to close the door on Sarah's Circle and walk away forever. What does it matter how good and beautiful are the visions that stir our imaginations when they take us into waters that appear too stormy for our frightened selves to navigate?

At times lonely, almost sick in spirit, I slip away to walk among those forebears who live in me and of whom it was written in the Book of Hebrews (chapter 11) that they said yes to God's call to create a new and different society. Even Sarah, whose namesake we are, is mentioned in Hebrews because in old age, in times as uncertain as our own, she had the courage to become pregnant. With my mind's eye I watch as she in awe caresses with worn hands a wondrously swollen belly. For a pensive moment I linger at her side, and then move on to gaze at Simone Weil sharing the grim fatigue of factory workers; to mount with Etty Hillesum the steps of that cattle car destined for Auschwitz; to stand with Martin Luther King that fateful day on a balcony in Memphis. The records say that each of them had an opportunity to turn back. As it was, they kept on for the sake of the new life moving in them, aware that their lives were connected to more than this world. Mincing no words, their stories recount the cruel ordeals they suffered in the service of their visions. The Book of Hebrews explains that this is how any of us becomes a son or daughter of God. The Gospels and scores of Scriptures make clear that the end of suffering, borne with grace, is a transformed life. If we keep this in mind as we set out to build Christ's alternative institution, whether it be a church or a home for street people, we will be enabled to give praise in all the circumstances that threaten to overwhelm us and make us feel that we are not up to the trials that we must undergo. The word from Hebrews is that these men and women of faith were also weak, and were given strength—though not in advance—to endure incredible hardship, even to being handed over to death.

In The Church of The Saviour we have a course of study on Servant Leadership to ponder these and similar matters. What we have not fully known is that we have no possibility of being servant leaders until our sufferings have swept away those personas that enable us to keep our griefs hidden and our pride intact. How did we ever think that we could be instructed by something other than our pain when it is written of Jesus that he was taught through his sufferings (Heb. 2:10)? Does it not also say in the Book of Hebrews that suffering will be part of our training (Heb. 12:9)? We should not push these Scriptures aside as masochistic. They state the way life is in this world; also they teach that, in some mysterious way, suffering is the great awakener. Those who do not turn away from suffering are redeemed and become the world's redeemers.

In his insightful book, *The Pain That Heals*, Martin Israel wrote:

> Only those who have passed through the valley of lonely suffering can be relied on to sustain their brothers in need.[63]

The sufferings we have known in Sarah's Circle and other missions of The Church of The Saviour are not of the heroic stature that would raise us above our contemporaries. We have not been driven out of our neighborhoods, sent to prison, stoned, tortured, or made penniless for our solidarity with the oppressed. Those things are happening to our brothers and sisters in Guatemala and South Africa, but they are not as yet our lot.

The sufferings we know come from the troubles we have with ourselves, as well as with others. We disappoint each other in so many ways, failing to live up to expectations, to confirm one another, or to give support when it is needed. We make inordinate demands on ourselves and on those around us. In all-unconscious ways we seek to control. We want our will to prevail. We ourselves do not want to be responsible for a work of any great size, but neither do we want to give to others the authority that would enable them to exercise responsibility. On some days the question of where the power lies has the potential of destroying the whole undertaking. We may talk eloquently about obedience to each other's gifts, but in reality we again and again trip over jealousy and envy, those two closet emotions. Then, too, there is the clash between those who settle easily for mediocrity and those who strive for perfection.

We pour our life's blood into our projects and become so identified with them that we cannot bear the critical word. Feeling paranoid and vulnerable we treat those who question us as though they were enemies, and push to the fringes of our life the ones with sufficient temerity to suggest that there might be a better way for us to be doing things. Our recovery from this diseased state is sometimes slow and not always in time to heal the damage done.

Of all our failures the greatest may be our inability to communicate what is in our hearts, because we do not know those hearts as well as we think we do. So much of what we say is misunderstood. We miss the messages that others claim we would have heard loud and clear if only we had been listening. What hurts the most, however, is to love and find our love not returned in kind, our presence overlooked, and our thoughts unattended, or so at times it seems. Despite a hundred sermons on forgiveness, we do not forgive easily, nor find ourselves easily forgiven. Forgiveness, we discover, is always harder than the sermons make it out to be. New life springing up in us is the fruit of forgiveness, but first comes the dying.

The sufferings in small groups and in small intentional

communities are not unlike the suffering known in marriages. Any serious covenant—and this is what membership in the church is—gives us immense difficulties to be overcome. We yearn to be loved and to love, but we are not practiced in loving, in the revealing of ourselves to one another. Once aware of this, we will be more tender with each other, more willing to be students, more tolerant of our bungling efforts at closeness.

As far as relationships are concerned, the human race is in an early stage. We are just beginning to understand that to love is difficult, must be learned, and will require long and hard work. The covenants we make with each other give the framework for an apprenticeship that not only will reveal to us our capacity to care, to imagine, and to create, but also will uncover the dark and destructive forces latent in us all. "I have," wrote Simone Weil, "the germ of all possible crimes, or nearly all, within me."[64] The evil in the world must be uncovered in our own hearts. They are the real battlegrounds. When we can receive into consciousness and feel the cruelty, the meanness, the indifference, all the evils that move in us, we take on the sins of the world, and become heirs with Christ.

The journey we make into ourselves is not in order that we think poorly of ourselves, be made humble and dependent, but in order that we touch our divinity—know firsthand that superior essence that dwells in us. You and I are called to vast things. We must mature, become ripe and full inside for our own sake, and for the sake of each other, and for God's sake. We must put aside our childish understandings of God and of Christianity. In the radical words of Nikos Kazantzakis, one of the world's recent prophets,

It is not God who will save us—it is we who will save God, by battling, by creating, and by transmuting matter into spirit.[65]

We are called to be "saviours of God." These are startling words. Are they heresy? Only if we keep ourselves locked into the dogmatism of outworn ages. Only if there is no evolutionary growth of the spirit. Only if we are suspect when we are emboldened to think new thoughts about God.

No longer able to fit God under old features, Kazantzakis struggled to give him a contemporary face. We can all be encouraged in that struggle by the apostle Peter's vision while he was praying on a housetop (Acts 10). In that vision the skies opened up and a sheet containing every kind of animal and bird was lowered down in front of him. A voice said to him, "Now, Peter; kill and eat!" Peter answered, "Certainly not, Lord; I have never yet eaten anything profane or unclean!" A second time the voice spoke to him, "What God has made clean, you have no right to call profane." This was repeated three times and then the container was drawn up to heaven again.

Peter struggled for an understanding of his vision and came to know that he was being told never again to draw a line between the secular and the religious. God's transcendent life was in the whole universe—in every atom and every cell, in every piece of matter and every soul. After that revelation Peter was free to visit a household of non-Jews, violating what hitherto were the principles for the extension of Christianity. He was flying in the face of the establishment, breaking with the way things had always been done to test a new way to be in the world. Cornelius, the man he went to visit, was also a contemplative, open and searching, willing himself to think new thoughts, and to take risks. The two men had to find in each other a kindred spirit.

Breaking bread with Cornelius, sitting at his table, sharing ideas and experiences, Peter was awed to see the spirit descend upon his host and family and friends. That same spirit poured afresh over him: "'The truth I have now come to realize,' he said, 'is that God does not have favorites, but that anybody of any nationality who fears God and does what is right is acceptable to him'" (Acts 10:34–35).

The story of Peter's visit with Cornelius gives us important information on the development of the infant church, but more important is the help the story gives in the formation of our own lives. We are told that Christianity is an evolutionary faith—that it can change and unfold in us. Peter gives us each courage to think, and question, and to be in conflict with things as they are. We are enabled to receive into our hearts new understandings of the gospel even though they will set us apart from the comfortable companionship of our sisters and brothers. When the news reached Jerusalem that Peter had accepted non-Jews into the Christian church there was no celebration of his crossing of a crucial dividing line. The apostles and others found the news disturbing. Peter had contradicted what they understood as the teachings of Christ. If what he had done was acceptable, Jesus was no longer the "Jewish Lord and Christ," but "Lord of all."

No wonder Peter was suspect. We all must fight in ourselves the tendency to exclusivity, and the apostles were no exception. Without knowing it they leveled against Peter the same charge that had been leveled against Jesus. "'This man,' they said, 'welcomes sinners and eats with them'" (Luke 15:3). "'He has gone to stay at a sinner's house,' they said" (Luke 19:8).

Out of the ensuing dispute the men who had been discipled by Jesus and who thought everything was in place learned that they had no dependable orthodoxy set in tablets of stone. They would have to use their own heads and hearts. Hour by hour, and day by day they would have to be instructed by the Spirit. For such tutoring we need a desert place, a rooftop, or a closet. One must cherish lonely places to be informed and grow rich in one's innermost heart. The poet Rilke wrote:

> I hold this to be the highest task of a bond between two people: that each should stand guard over the solitude of the other. For, if it lies in the nature of indifference and of the crowd to recognize no solitude, then love and friendship are there for the purpose of continually providing the opportunity for solitude.[66]

The time apart enables us to relax into ourselves, allow into consciousness all those unacceptable thoughts which need a hearing even when they threaten to turn our little worlds upside down and make us outcasts. The solitude is for dreaming dreams and seeing visions. The solitude lets us be contemplatives, relinquishing our tight hold on self, that by our free consent Christ may dwell in us. In the words of Paul:

> . . . it is no longer I who live,
> but Christ who lives in me.
> Galatians 2:20, RSV

For a long time the mystics and the poets—the people who fall into trances on rooftops—have been trying to tell us that we must put away our childish understanding of God's omnipotence. Our lives are not made safe, secure, and comfortable when we surrender them to Christ. He does not give us the money we need for the good projects we have in mind, or whistle up from some corner of the earth the person that will help us out of our difficulties. He does not save our lives let alone provide us with all those things we think we need for a secure and satisfying lifestyle.

The word is quite different. When we reach inward to ourselves we realize our own spirituality; we find ourselves willing to take risks we were afraid to take, willing to be out on a limb all alone, willing to give up the comforts to which we have been clinging. We find ourselves able to receive new truth, and to have our understanding of old truths expanded.

Our souls grow into their full stature. We are empowered to write and speak and act without being deterred by "What will become of us?" or "What will they think?" But it is more than what we say and what we do that undergoes change. Our whole lives proclaim Christ. The call so long resisted becomes irresistible. We see our task in a new light. We understand what it means to become responsible.

In all the cherished pages of Etty Hillesum's journal the words that hold the most meaning for our age may be those that record one of her conversations with God:

I shall try to help You, God, to stop my strength ebbing away, though I cannot vouch for it in advance. But one thing is becoming increasingly clear to me: that You cannot help us, that we must help You to help ourselves. And that is all we can manage these days and also all that really matters: that we safeguard that little piece of You, God, in ourselves. And perhaps in others as well. Alas, there doesn't seem to be much You Yourself can do about our circumstances, about our lives. Neither do I hold You responsible. You cannot help us but we must help You and defend Your dwelling place inside us to the last.[67]

If these words were understood, they would change the way Christianity is preached in the churches and, even more importantly, the way we relate to God and to one another.

Nikolai Berdyaev, who could not think of divine love except in terms of sacrificial love "of an eternal movement toward the loved one," wrote:

God is freedom; he is not Lord, but Liberator; he is the Saviour and Liberator from the slavery of the world. . . .[68]

God is spirit, and he acts within the order of freedom and not of objectified necessity. His activity cannot be understood in naturalistic terms. He is present not in external things and happenings, to which we attach divine names and in which we perceive a divine purpose, not in the power or powers of this world, but in truth, beauty, love, freedom, and creativity. This precludes all conceptions which make of him the subject of power and almighty influences. God has no power: he has less power than a policeman. Power is a social and not a religious phenomenon.[69]

In one of his last letters from prison Dietrich Bonhoeffer wrote words which were perplexing to many of us who read them when they were first published, and which now seem clearer as I go back and reread them:

. . . our coming of age leads us to a true recognition of our situation before God. God would have us know that we must live as men who manage our lives without him. The God who is with us is the God who forsakes us (Mark 15:34). The God who lets us live in the world without the working hypothesis of God is the God before whom we stand continually. Before God and with God we live without God. God lets himself be pushed out of the world on to the cross. He is weak and powerless in the world, and that is precisely the way, the only way, in which he is with us and helps us. Matthew 8:17 makes it quite clear that Christ helps us, not by virtue of his omnipotence, but by virtue of his weakness and suffering.[70]

Undoubtedly in his own great distress Bonhoeffer had begun to question the common interpretations of God's omnipotence. Helpless to do anything about his own circumstances he was led into an experience of God's powerlessness and suffering that threw new light on the Scriptures. He wrote that if we could put away a false conception of God, the way would be opened to "seeing the God of the Bible, who wins power and space in the world by his weakness."[71]

Bonhoeffer hoped to develop these thoughts in a book that would have only three chapters. His outline for chapter 2 contained these sentences:

"Jesus is there only for others." His "being there for others" is the experience of transcendence. It is only this "being there for others," maintained till death, that is the ground of his omnipotence, omniscience, and omnipresence. Faith is participation in this being of Jesus (incarnation, cross, and resurrection). Our relation to God is not a "religious" relationship to the highest, most powerful, and best Being imaginable—that is not authentic transcendence—but our relation to God is a new life in "existence for others," through participation in the being of Jesus. . . .[72]

His very last letter from prison summons us "to share in God's sufferings at the hands of a godless world."[73] In that letter he asked the question, "But what does this life look like, this participation in the powerlessness of God in the world? I will write about that next time, I hope."[74] There was no next time.

Without any further help from Bonhoeffer you and I must

struggle for a new understanding of the man and woman of faith in today's world. We do not have to be afraid to ponder this matter. God is not endangered when we think about what it means to grow into a mature spirituality, a mature Christianity. "Christ likes us to prefer truth to him," wrote Simone Weil, "because, before being Christ, he is truth. If one turns aside from him to go toward the truth, one will not go far before falling into his arms."[75] Complacency, indifference, smugness, suspicion, and narrowness are what place God in jeopardy—our slowness to know that the God who hears our cries and who gathers us into his arms is also the crucified God, the God who is crying out to us, the God who needs us to become responsible.

> For I called and you would not answer,
> I spoke and you would not listen.
> > Isaiah 65:12

Once more the words of the poet, Nikos Kazantzakis:

My God struggles on without certainty. Will he conquer? Will he be conquered? Nothing in the Universe is certain. He flings himself into uncertainty; he gambles all his destiny at every moment.

He clings to warm bodies; he has no other bulwark. He shouts for help; he proclaims a mobilization throughout the Universe.

It is our duty, on hearing his Cry, to run under his flag, to fight by his side, to be lost or to be saved with him.

God is imperiled. He is not almighty, that we may cross our hands, waiting for certain victory. He is not all-holy, that we may wait trustingly for him to pity and to save us.

Within the province of our ephemeral flesh all of God is imperiled. He cannot be saved unless we save him with our own struggles, nor can we be saved unless he is saved.

We are one. From the blind worm in the depths of the ocean to the endless arena of the Galaxy, only one person struggles and is imperiled: You. And within your small and earthen breast only one thing struggles and is imperiled: the Universe.[76]

An underlying theme in these writers is God's belief in us. God has entrusted the world to us. God has made us guardians of divinity. No matter how inadequate or clumsy any of us is, or how low any one of us may fall, we can believe in each other because God believes in us.

The poet Denise Levertov meditated on the symbol "Lamb of God" and expressed what well may be our own astonishment at the disclosure in those three words:

> Given that lambs
> are infant sheep, that sheep
> are afraid and foolish, and lack
> the means of self-protection, having
> neither rage nor claws,
> venom nor cunning,
> what then
> is this "Lamb of God"?
> . . . .
> What terror lies concealed
> in strangest words, O *lamb*
> *of God that taketh away*
> *the Sins of the World*: an innocence
>   smelling of ignorance,
>   born in bloody snowdrifts,
>   licked by forebearing
> dogs more intelligent than its entire flock put together?
>
>   God then,
>   encompassing all things, is
>   defenseless? Omnipotence
>   has been tossed away, reduced
>   to a wisp of damp wool?
>
>   And we,
>   frightened, bored, wanting
> only to sleep till catastrophe
> has raged, clashed, seethed and gone by without us,
>   wanting then
> to awaken in quietude without remembrance of agony,

we who in shamefaced private hope
has looked to be plucked from fire and given
a bliss we deserved for having imagined it,

is it implied that *we*
must protect this perversely weak
animal whose muzzle's nudgings
suppose there is milk to be found in us?
Must hold to our icy hearts
a shivering God? . . .[77]

38

A Dying and a Birth

Once I wrote that Sarah's Circle had the potential of pouring fresh energy into the streets and into our society. I must have only half-believed it because now I look on in awe to see it happening. God is greening a building and greening the people who live in it and those of us who touch them.

Hard to think back to those months not so long ago, when I wanted to walk out of Sarah's Circle, never to return. The odds against resuscitating the building that was Sarah's Circle and turning our own lives around seemed too great. The intergenerational community we found in our circle included not only the frail and vulnerable old, but drug dealers, alcoholics, battered wives, and abused children. Also in that circle were unsung heroes and heroines of deteriorating buildings and ghetto streets who, in the midst of ruins, struggle day in and day out for a decent and meaningful life. Moreover, those of us who are the founders of Sarah's Circle were there, trying to stay faithful to the vision, but oftentimes stressed out, not knowing fully how to cope, where to turn, or what to do next—disappointed in ourselves and in each other.

How did the healing begin to happen? I cannot say for sure, but I think a wind was blowing in the darkness of our despair— in all those times when we were forced to draw apart and make descent into that fiery furnace that is in each of us. I doubt if anyone is healed and, in turn, becomes a healer without facing and mastering the Devil who stokes the fires of that furnace.

How did the healing begin to happen? I cannot say for sure, but I think a wind was blowing in the hundreds of conversations that went on in the lobby, in the apartments of the residents, and on the sidewalk. I think it was blowing when we searched through the garbage dumped into our courtyard in order to determine the identity of the offender, and again, later in the day, when we talked with him.

I think the wind was blowing when a tenant said to Sheila, "Leon urinated in the stairwell of Sarah's Circle. What are you going to do about it?"

"I don't know," said our director of programming; but a few minutes later gentle Sheila was out on the street corner where Leon was standing with the group of men who gather there each day. "I don't want to embarrass you in front of your friends," she said, "but you urinated in our building stairwell. I don't want you ever to do that again."

"You didn't see me," he said.

"No," she replied, "but I believe it was you."

"I'll drop by your office in a little while," he answered.

An hour later he was in her office. "I'm not going to say whether I did it, or I didn't do it," he said, "but I promise you I won't do it again." With that he held out his hand. "I respect you," he said. "I respect you and what you are doing here. I wasn't drinking for two months, and then I went back to it. Watch, I'm going to stop again."

I think a wind was blowing on all those afternoons when we gathered in our women's group, learning over the months that we could trust each other, giving up the masks of respectability that we were wearing to share our secrets and make the discovery that this is how we become sisters. At one meeting, after telling some of our troubles, we closed our eyes and went down to Jerusalem's ancient Wailing Wall, and put our pain into moans, joining that great company of men and women who over the centuries have gathered at that wall to make petition to the One who is able to save.

How did the healing begin to happen? I cannot say for sure, but I know a wind was blowing through the art classes, the trips to galleries, the reading of the Scriptures against the hard reality of Sarah's Circle.

Many times we found it difficult to stay afloat in the stormy waters that threatened to engulf us. We did not know at the time the significance of the passage we were making. Only in looking back were we given the name of the Sea that had not overwhelmed us. I will tell from now until the end of my days the story of our deliverance—how God went before us, a cloud by day and a pillar of fire by night—and how it was I came to know that we had arrived at Christmas.

The circumstances were no more extraordinary than they probably seemed to an innkeeper on that first Christmas. The mission group members were gathered with the tenants in the fourth floor apartment we have reserved for our times together. Twenty or more of us were crowded into a room to watch on our new television set the film *Out of Africa*. In the dark of that room, looking at the incredibly beautiful landscape of Africa, my mind drifted away from the film to reflect on the wonder of the simple gathering. We were poor, we were rich; we were black, we were white; and God had made us a people. I knew it was Christmas because I was in love with this people, and felt my love returned—which is what it must mean to be God's people and to dance Sarah's Circle.

When tomorrow comes, we can begin to walk the long road to Calvary and, God willing, to Easter Day. Then will come a new Annunciation and a new waiting. But now it is Christmas!

Notes

1. Hildegard of Bingen, *Illuminations of Hildegard of Bingen* with commentary by Matthew Fox (Santa Fe: Bear & Co., Inc., 1985), pp. 32–33. Used by permission.

2. Gabriele Uhlein, *Meditations with TM Hildegard of Bingen* (Santa Fe: Bear & Co., Inc., 1982), p. 110.

3. Peter Stitt, *The World's Hieroglyphic Beauty: Five American Poets* (Athens, GA: University of Georgia Press, 1985), pp. 40–41.

4. Wilfried Daim, "The First Revolutionary," *The Center Magazine*, September–October, 1972, pp. 38–39.

5. Ibid., p. 39.

6. Lord Byron, "The Prisoner of Chillon," *Byron's Poetry* (New York: W. W. Norton & Co., Inc., 1978), p. 115.

7. Katherine L. Bates, "O Beautiful for Spacious Skies," *Pilgrim Hymnal* (Long Island, NY: Pilgrim Press, 1931), p. 440.

8. Maurice Nicoll, *Psychological Commentaries on the Teaching of G. I. Gurdjieff and P. D. Ouspensky* (London: Vincent Stuart & John M. Watkins, Ltd., 1970), p. 25.

9. Martin Buber, *The Writing of Martin Buber*, selected and introduced by Will Herberg (New York: New American Library, 1974), p. 314.

10. Rita Reif, "Assessing the Shaker Style," *New York Times*, 8 June 1986.

11. Edna St. Vincent Millay, "God's World," *Modern American Poetry, Modern British Poetry: A Critical Anthology*, ed. Louis Untermeyer (New York: Harcourt Brace and Company, 1919), p. 492.

12. Ken Kesey, *One Flew Over the Cuckoo's Nest*. Text and Criticism, ed. John C. Pratt (New York: Viking Press, 1973), pp. 349–50.

13. Ibid., p. 350.

14. Ibid., pp. 351–52.

15. Anne Morrow Lindbergh, "Even," *The Unicorn and Other Poems* (New York: Random House, Pantheon Books, 1972), p. 14. Used by permission.

16. Thomas Merton, *The Asian Journal* (New York: New Directions Press, 1968), p. 338.

17. Yaffa Eliah, "No Time for Advice," *Hasidic Tales of the Holocaust* (New York: Avon Books, 1982), pp. 57–59.

18. Hyemeyoshsts Storm, *Seven Arrows* (New York: Harper & Row, 1972), p. 7.

19. Joel Porte, ed., *Emerson in His Journals* (Cambridge, MA, and London: The Belknap Press of Harvard University Press, 1982), p. 241.

20. Sara Teasdale, *Rivers to the Sea* (New York: The MacMillan Co., 1923), p. 63.

21. Victor Cohn, "Sometimes, You Have to Be Pushy," *The Washington Post*, 28 August 1985, p. 8.

22. Larry Thompson, "Age Won't Kill You," *The Washington Post*, 9 July 1986.

23. Alex Comfort, *A Good Age* (New York: Crown Publishers, Inc., 1976), p. 12.

24. Ibid., p. 30.

25. Ibid., p. 16.

26. Ibid.

27. Frederick Buechner, *Peculiar Treasures: A Biblical Who's Who* (New York: Harper & Row, Pubs., 1979), p. 153.

28. Matthew Fox, *A Spiritually Named Compassion, and the Healing of the Global Village, Humpty Dumpty, and Us* (Minneapolis: Winston Press, 1979).

29. William Blake, *The Portable Blake* (New York: The Viking Press, Inc., 1946), p. 655.

30. *Grimms' Fairy Tales*, No. 1, "The Frog King."

31. Joseph Campbell, *The Hero with a Thousand Faces*, Bollingen Series XVII. (Princeton: Princeton University Press, copyright 1949, © renewed by Princeton University Press), p. 218. Used by permission.

32. Blake, "The Tyger," *The Portable Blake*, p. 109.

33. Robert Bridges, ed., *Poems of Gerard Manley Hopkins* (New York and London: Oxford University Press, [1918] 1948), p. 112.

34. John Steinbeck, *Grapes of Wrath* (New York: Penguin Books, 1977).

35. Campbell, *The Hero with a Thousand Faces*, p. 72.

36. Robert J. Clements, ed., *Michelangelo: A Self-Portrait* (New York: New York University Press, 1968), p. 144.

37. Louis Ormont and Herbert S. Strean, *The Practice of Conjoint Therapy: Combining Individual and Group Treatment* (New York: Human Sciences Press, 1978), p. 112.

38. Blake, "The Poison Tree," *The Portable Blake*, p. 114.

39. Blake, *The Portable Blake*, p. 25.

40. Simone Weil, *Waiting for God* (New York: Harper & Row, 1973), p. 115.

41. Norman Cousins, *Anatomy of an Illness* (New York: W. W. Norton & Co., 1979), pp. 153-54. Used by permission of the publisher.

42. Francis Moore Lappé, *Diet for a Small Planet* (New York: Ballantine Books, 1971).

43. Boyce Rensberger, "The Nature-Nurture Debate from Samoa to Sociology." *Science*, April, 1983, pp. 36–37.

44. Merlin R. Carothers, *Power in Praise* (Escondido, CA: Carothers Co., 1972).

45. ———, *Prison to Praise* (Escondido, CA: Carothers Co., 1970).

46. John J. L. Mood, ed., *Rilke on Love and Other Difficulties: Translations and Consideration of Rainer Maria Rilke* (New York: W. W. Norton & Co., 1975).

47. H. A. Williams, *True Wilderness* (Philadelphia and New York: J. P. Lippincott Co., 1965), p. 70.

48. Denise Levertov, *The Poet in the World* (New York: New Directions,

© 1973 Denise Levertov Goodman), p. 104. Reprinted by permission of New Directions Publishing Corporation.

49. Thomas Merton, "The Goal of the Ascetic Life," *The Mystic Life* (Chappaqua, NY: Electronic Paperbacks, © 1976 Trustees of the Merton Legacy Fund), tape 3, side B.

50. William Shannon, "Contemplation as Total Awareness," *Agape*, Fall 1983, p. 4.

51. Juliana of Norwich, *Revelations of Divine Love* (Garden City, NY: Image Books, 1977), p. 88.

52. Nikolai Berdyaev, *Dream and Reality: An Essay in Autobiography*, trans. Katharine Lampert (New York: The Macmillan Co., n.d.), pp. 204–5.

53. ———, *The Destiny of Man* (New York: Harper & Row Pubs., n.d.), p. 152.

54. Madeleine L'Engle, *The Irrational Season* (New York: Seabury Press, 1979), p. 27.

55. Etty Hillesum, *An Interrupted Life: The Diaries of Etty Hillesum, 1941–1943*, trans. Arno Pomerans (New York: Random House, Pantheon Books, 1983), p. 1. Used by permission.

56. Ibid., p. 205.
57. Ibid., p. 27.
58. Ibid., p. 151.
59. Ibid., p. 198.
60. Ibid., p. 173.
61. Ibid., p. 198.
62. Ibid., p. 199.

63. Martin Israel, *The Pain That Heals* (London: Hodder and Stoughton, 1981), p. 24.

64. Weil, *Waiting for God*, p. 48.

65. Nikos Kazantzakis, *The Saviors of God, Spiritual Exercises* (New York: Simon & Schuster, 1960), p. 106. Used by permission.

66. Mood, *Rilke on Love*.

67. Hillesum, *An Interrupted Life*, p. 151.

68. Berdyaev, *Dream and Reality*, p. 175.

69. Ibid., pp. 177–78.

70. Dietrich Bonhoeffer, *Letters and Papers from Prison* (New York: Macmillan Publishing Co., 1972), pp. 360–61. Reprinted with permission of Macmillan Publishing Company. Copyright © 1972 SCM Press, Ltd.

71. Ibid., p. 361.
72. Ibid., p. 381.
73. Ibid., p. 361.
74. Ibid., p. 362.

75. Weil, *Waiting for God*, p. 69.

76. Kazantzakis, *Saviors of God*, pp. 104–5. Used by permission.

77. Denise Levertov, "Mass for the Day of St. Thomas Didymus," *Candles in Babylon* (New York: New Directions, Copyright © 1982 by Denise Levertov Goodman), pp. 113–14. Reprinted by permission of New Directions Publishing Corporation.